"Dancing with Dodos"

A Fun Guide to Understanding Everyone

(Even the Weirdos)

by

Orion Windsor

www.quanttumhealing.com

Dedication

To my amazing children Oscar and Evie and my friends who've been by my side when times were hard, " You know who you are".

Thank you. Without your support and patience, I would have never achieved my dream.

First Printing: 2024

QuanTTum Healing

Contents

Foreword

Greetings, luminous souls,

Welcome to a journey into the vibrant world of personalities! In today's interconnected and fast-paced world, understanding ourselves and those around us is more crucial than ever. This book, filled with insights, practical exercises, and real-life examples, is your companion to unravelling the mysteries of human behaviour through the lens of personality types.

As you embark on these pages, you'll discover the fascinating spectrum of personalities, each with its own distinct traits—Lion's (Dominant), Parrot's (Influential), Dolphins (Stable), and Owls (Conscientious). Through engaging exercises and reflective prompts, you'll explore how these traits shape our thoughts, actions, and interactions in everyday scenarios.

Why does it matter? Because understanding personality types isn't just about categorising people; it's about enhancing communication, fostering empathy, and building stronger relationships. Whether you're navigating office dynamics, nurturing friendships, or seeking harmony in romantic relationships, this book equips you with practical tools to navigate the diverse personalities you encounter.

Through expert interviews, case studies, and success stories, you'll witness firsthand how insights into personality dynamics can transform workplaces, enrich personal connections, and pave the way for personal growth. You'll learn to adapt your communication style, leverage strengths, and navigate conflicts with confidence and grace.

Above all, this book invites you to embark on a journey of self-discovery and growth. By embracing the diversity of personalities around us, we not only deepen our understanding of others but also unlock our own potential to thrive in a world where human connection and understanding reign supreme.

So, let's dive in, explore the animal of personalities, and embark on a transformative journey towards better relationships, enriched experiences, and a more harmonious world.

Warm regards,

Orion Windsor

Chapter 1: The Animal Kingdom of Personalities

Overview of Personality Types

Welcome to the vibrant world of personality types! Understanding different personality traits is like having a key to unlock better communication, stronger relationships, and greater self-awareness. In this book, we explore four primary personality types, each represented by an animal that highlights its unique characteristics: Lion's (Dominant), Parrot's (Influential), Dolphin (Stable), and Owl (Conscientious). Let's dive into each of these fascinating personality types and see what makes them tick.

Lion's (Dominant)

Traits and Characteristics:

- **Bold and Decisive:** Lion's are natural leaders who take charge of situations. They are assertive, confident, and quick to make decisions.
- **Goal-Oriented:** They focus on results and efficiency, often pushing themselves and others to achieve ambitious targets.
- **Competitive:** Lion's thrive on competition and are driven by challenges. They enjoy being in control and can be quite persuasive.

Why It Matters: Understanding lion's helps in recognizing their need for control and efficiency. Effective communication with Lion's involves being direct, concise, and respecting their time and goals. Appreciating their drive can lead to better collaboration and mutual respect.

Parrot's (Influential)

Traits and Characteristics:

- **Energetic and Sociable:** Parrot's are the life of the party. They are enthusiastic, optimistic, and excellent at building relationships.
- **Persuasive:** With their charm and communication skills, Parrot's can easily influence and motivate others.
- **Creative and Spontaneous:** They bring creativity and excitement to projects, often thinking outside the box and coming up with innovative ideas.

Why It Matters: Recognizing the energy and creativity of Parrot's helps in harnessing their enthusiasm for positive outcomes. Communicating with Parrot's involves being engaging, open, and supportive of their ideas. Their influence can inspire and energise teams.

Dolphin (Stable)

Traits and Characteristics:

- **Patient and Reliable:** Dolphins are the glue that holds teams together. They are supportive, dependable, and excellent listeners.
- **Calm and Cooperative:** They prefer harmony and avoid conflicts, often acting as mediators in tense situations.
- **Loyal:** Dolphins value relationships and are deeply loyal to their friends, family, and colleagues.

Why It Matters: Understanding Dolphins' need for stability and harmony helps in fostering a supportive environment. Effective communication with Dolphins involves being patient, showing appreciation, and providing reassurance. Their reliability and cooperative nature are invaluable in maintaining team cohesion.

Owl (Conscientious)

Traits and Characteristics:

- **Detail-Oriented and Analytical:** Owls are meticulous and thorough. They focus on accuracy, data, and logical reasoning.
- **Organised:** They excel at planning and organising tasks, ensuring everything is done correctly and efficiently.
- **Critical Thinkers:** Owls approach problems with a logical mindset, often questioning and analysing to find the best solutions.

Why It Matters: Recognizing the precision and analytical skills of Owls helps in appreciating their thoroughness and attention to detail. Communicating with Owls involves being clear, providing detailed information, and respecting their need for accuracy. Their critical thinking can enhance decision-making processes.

Why Understanding Personality Types Matters

Understanding these personality types goes beyond simple categorization. It's about appreciating the diverse strengths each type brings to the table and learning how to interact effectively with different personalities. By recognizing and adapting to these traits, we can improve communication, reduce conflicts, and build stronger, more harmonious relationships both personally and professionally.

As we explore the Animal world of personality types, remember that everyone embodies a unique blend of these traits. This book will guide you in identifying, understanding, and leveraging these traits to enhance your interactions and relationships. Get ready to dive deeper into each personality type, discover practical tips, and engage in exercises that will help you apply these insights in your daily life. Welcome to a transformative journey of self-discovery and better connections

Lion's (Dominant)

Lion's are the go-getters of the world. They're assertive, decisive, and love taking charge. Think of them as the Lion's of the personality jungle.

Traits and Characteristics:

- **Driven and Goal-Oriented:** Lion's are always on the move, aiming to achieve their next big goal.
- **Confident and Competitive:** They exude confidence and thrive in competitive environments.
- **Direct and Decisive:** They prefer clear, straightforward communication and quick decisions.

Real-Life Examples:

- The CEO who built a company from scratch.
- The coach who pushes their team to victory.
- The friend who always organises group activities and sets the plan.

Strengths:

- Excellent leaders who can motivate others.
- Skilled at making quick decisions and taking action.

Challenges:

- Can be perceived as aggressive or intimidating.
- May overlook others' feelings in their pursuit of goals.

Parrot's (Influential)

Parrot's are the social butterflies, full of energy and always ready to have fun. They're the parrots of the group, chatting away and spreading cheer.

Traits and Characteristics:

- **Optimistic and Enthusiastic:** Parrot's bring positive energy wherever they go.
- **Persuasive and Sociable:** They have a knack for convincing others and love being around people.
- **Creative and Spontaneous:** They think outside the box and thrive on spontaneity.

Real-Life Examples:

- The friend who is always the life of the party.
- The marketer who can sell anything to anyone.
- The colleague who keeps the office atmosphere lively.

Strengths:

- Great at networking and building relationships.
- Inspire others with their enthusiasm and creativity.

Challenges:

- May struggle with details and follow-through.
- Can be seen as disorganised or overly talkative.

Dolphin (Stable)

Dolphins are the peacekeepers, providing stability and support. They're the turtles, slow and steady, ensuring everyone feels safe and comfortable.

Traits and Characteristics:

- **Patient and Reliable:** Dolphins are dependable and always there when you need them.
- **Good Listeners and Supportive:** They excel at listening and offering support.
- **Loyal and Team-Oriented:** They value relationships and work well in teams.

Real-Life Examples:

- The friend who is always there to lend an ear.
- The nurse who provides compassionate care.
- The teacher who patiently guides their students.

Strengths:

- Excellent at maintaining harmony and building trust.
- Provide consistent and reliable support.

Challenges:

- May resist change and avoid conflict.
- Can be perceived as passive or indecisive.

<h1 style="text-align:center">Owl (Conscientious)</h1>

Owls are the thinkers and planners, focused on precision and accuracy. They're the owls, wise and meticulous, always analysing and perfecting.

Traits and Characteristics:

- **Analytical and Detail-Oriented:** Owls love details and excel at problem-solving.
- **Organised and Methodical:** They prefer structure environments and clear procedures.
- **Cautious and Risk-Averse:** They think carefully before making decisions.

Real-Life Examples:

- The accountant who ensures everything balances.
- The scientist who meticulously conducts experiments.
- The friend who plans every detail of a trip.

Strengths:

- Highly organised and excellent at planning.
- Provide valuable insights through careful analysis.

Challenges:

- Can be overly critical or perfectionistic.
- May struggle with spontaneity and quick decisions.

Why It Matters

Understanding personality types isn't just for psychologists; it's a practical tool for everyday life. Here's why it's crucial:

1. **Improved Communication:**
   - **Tailor Your Approach:** Knowing someone's type helps you communicate in a way they'll understand and appreciate. For example, be direct with Lion's, enthusiastic with Parrot's, patient with Dolphins, and detailed with Owls.
   - **Reduce Misunderstandings:** Recognizing different communication styles can prevent conflicts and misunderstandings.

2. **Enhanced Relationships:**
   - **Build Stronger Connections:** Understanding what makes others tick can deepen your relationships. You'll know how to support a Dolphin friend or motivate a Lion's colleague.
   - **Resolve Conflicts Effectively:** When conflicts arise, knowing the personality dynamics can help you navigate and resolve issues more effectively.

3. **Personal Growth:**
   - **Self-Awareness:** Understanding your own personality type can highlight your strengths and areas for improvement.
   - **Flexibility:** Learning about different types encourages you to adapt and become more versatile in your interactions.

4. **Team Dynamics:**
    - ○ **Balanced Teams:** In work or personal projects, knowing each member's type can help you create balanced teams that leverage everyone's strengths.
    - ○ **Increased Productivity:** Teams that understand and appreciate personality differences are often more cohesive and productive.

This chapter sets the stage for our Animal journey through human interactions. Get ready to explore, laugh, and learn as we dive deeper into each personality type and how to dance with them in the chapters to come.

Chapter 2: Meet the Lions: The Fierce Leaders

Welcome to the realm of the Lion's! These bold and decisive individuals are the leaders of the personality spectrum. They might seem intimidating at times, but understanding their motivations and behaviours can help you get along with them and even harness their strengths to your advantage.

Traits and Characteristics: Bold, Decisive, and Often Intimidating

Lion's are the movers and shakers of the world. Here's a closer look at what makes them tick:

Bold:

- **Fearless:** Lion's aren't afraid to take risks. They're the first to jump into a new venture or challenge.
- **Assertive:** They know what they want and aren't shy about going after it. Their assertiveness can sometimes come off as aggression, but it's usually just their way of ensuring things get done.

Decisive:

- **Quick Decision-Makers:** Lion's excel at making decisions swiftly. They don't waste time over-analyzing; they assess the situation, weigh the options, and act.
- **Goal-Oriented:** They have a clear vision of their goals and the steps needed to achieve them. Their decisiveness helps them stay on track and avoid distractions.

Intimidating:

- **High Expectations:** Lion's often hold themselves and others to high standards. They expect everyone to keep up with their pace and may become impatient with those who don't.
- **Strong Presence:** Their confidence and assertiveness can be overwhelming, especially to those who are more reserved or sensitive.

Real-Life Examples: Your No-Nonsense Manager, the Driven Entrepreneur

Lion's are everywhere, and they often stand out in any crowd due to their dynamic nature. Here are a few common scenarios where you might encounter a Lion's:

Your No-Nonsense Manager:

- **In the Workplace:** This manager is always on the move, pushing their team to meet tight deadlines and high standards. They don't have time for small talk; they want results.
- **Communication Style:** They prefer brief, to-the-point conversations. Don't expect lengthy explanations or emotional discussions—just the facts and the action plan.

The Driven Entrepreneur:

- **In Business:** Entrepreneurs often embody the Lion's personality. They're the ones who start companies from scratch, take big risks, and aren't afraid of failure.
- **Leadership Style:** They inspire through their vision and determination. They expect their team to share their passion and drive, and they won't hesitate to make tough decisions to keep the business moving forward.

The Assertive Friend:

- **In Social Settings:** This friend is the one who always plans the outings and decides where the group will go. They're confident, outspoken, and sometimes come off as domineering.
- **Interaction Style:** They appreciate honesty and directness. Be straightforward with them, and they'll respect you for it.

Worksheet: Identify the Lion's in Your Life

Now, it's time to identify the Lion's around you. This worksheet will help you pinpoint these bold, decisive individuals and understand how to interact with them more effectively.

Step 1: List People You Know Think about the people in your life—friends, family, colleagues, and acquaintances. Write down the names of those who stand out as bold and decisive.

Step 2: Evaluate Their Traits For each person on your list, consider the following questions:

- Do they make decisions quickly and confidently?
- Are they goal-oriented and driven?
- Do they come off as assertive or even intimidating at times?
- Do they have high expectations of themselves and others?

Step 3: Note Your Interactions Reflect on your interactions with these individuals:

- How do they communicate with you? (Direct and to the point, or detailed and explanatory?)
- How do you feel when you interact with them? (Motivated, intimidated, inspired?)
- What strategies have you used to get along with them?

Step 4: Plan Your Approach Based on your reflections, develop a strategy for interacting with the Lion's in your life:

- **Be Direct:** Avoid beating around the bush. State your points clearly and concisely.
- **Show Confidence:** Match their assertiveness with your own confidence. Stand your ground respectfully.
- **Respect Their Time:** Lion's appreciate efficiency. Keep meetings and conversations focused and productive.
- **Acknowledge Their Drive:** Recognize their achievements and goals. Show that you respect their ambition.

Example Worksheet Entry:

Person: Sarah (Manager)

- **Traits:** Quick decision-maker, high standards, confident.
- **Interactions:** Prefers brief meetings, appreciates straightforward communication.
- **Plan:** Prepare concise reports, be clear and direct in emails, acknowledge her leadership and drive.

By identifying the Lion's in your life and understanding their traits, you can improve your interactions and build more effective, respectful relationships. Remember, Lion's thrive on challenge and action, so show them you can keep up with their pace and drive. Happy identifying!

Chapter 3: Handling Lions without Losing Your Head

Now that you've identified the Lion's in your life, it's time to master the art of interacting with them. While Lion's can be intense and demanding, understanding how to communicate effectively with them will help you build a stronger, more respectful relationship. This chapter provides practical tips, dos and don'ts, and a fun role-playing exercise to practise your new skills.

Communication Tips: Be Direct and Concise

Lion's appreciate efficiency and clarity in communication. Here's how you can make your interactions with them smoother:

Be Direct:

- **Get to the Point:** Avoid long-winded explanations. Lion's prefer you to cut to the chase. For example, instead of saying, "I was thinking that maybe we could possibly consider changing the approach to the project," say, "We should change the project approach to X."
- **State Your Intentions Clearly:** Make your requests or opinions clear from the outset. Lion's don't like guessing games or ambiguity.

Be Concise:

- **Keep it Brief:** Use as few words as possible to convey your message. They'll appreciate not having to sift through unnecessary details.
- **Highlight Key Points:** When presenting information, focus on the most critical aspects first. Use bullet points or summaries to make it easier for them to grasp the main ideas quickly.

Provide Solutions, Not Problems:

- **Come Prepared:** When discussing issues, always bring potential solutions. Lion's respect proactive problem-solving and dislike hearing about problems without a proposed fix.
- **Be Results-Oriented:** Frame your communication around outcomes and results. Lion's are goal-driven and will respond better to discussions centred on achieving specific objectives.

Dos and Don'ts

To navigate your interactions with Lion's effectively, keep these dos and don'ts in mind:

Dos:

- **Do Show Respect for Their Time:** Lion's value efficiency. Ensure meetings and conversations are productive and to the point.
- **Do Acknowledge Their Achievements:** Recognize and appreciate their accomplishments and hard work. A little acknowledgment goes a long way.
- **Do Be Confident:** Match their assertiveness with your own confidence. Stand your ground respectfully and show that you can keep up.
- **Do Focus on Results:** Frame discussions around goals and outcomes. Lion's are driven by success and achievement.

Don'ts:

- **Don't Beat Around the Bush:** Avoid vague language and unnecessary details. Be clear and direct in your communication.
- **Don't Take Their Intensity Personally:** Lion's can come off as aggressive or impatient. Understand that it's their way of driving results, not a personal attack.
- **Don't Waste Their Time:** Keep interactions focused and efficient. Avoid rambling or veering off-topic.
- **Don't Undermine Their Authority:** Respect their leadership and decisions. Disagreements should be handled with tact and respect.

Fun Exercise: Role-Play Scenarios with a Lion's

Practising your new skills through role-playing can be a fun and effective way to prepare for real-life interactions with Lion's. Here are some scenarios to try out with a friend, colleague, or even by yourself:

Scenario 1: Pitching a New Idea to Your Lion's Manager

1. **Setup:**
   - You have a new project idea that you believe will improve the company's performance.
   - Your manager (the Lion's) is known for their no-nonsense attitude and preference for direct communication.

2. **Role-Play:**
   - **You:** "I have a proposal that will increase our sales by 15% in the next quarter. Here's a brief outline of the strategy."
   - **Manager:** "Go on."
   - **You:** "The plan involves targeting a new market segment and leveraging our current resources to maximise efficiency. The key steps are outlined here in three points: [Briefly list points]. I believe this can be implemented within the next two months."

3. **Objective:**
   - Present your idea clearly and concisely.
   - Focus on the potential outcomes and benefits.
   - Be prepared to answer questions directly and confidently.

Scenario 2: Resolving a Conflict with a Lion's Colleague

1. **Setup:**
   - You and a Lion's colleague have a disagreement about the direction of a project.
   - The goal is to resolve the conflict without escalating it.

2. **Role-Play:**
   - **You:** "I'd like to discuss our different views on the project. My main concern is the timeline. Here's why I think extending the deadline could benefit us: [Briefly explain]."
   - **Colleague:** "We need to stick to the original schedule."
   - **You:** "I understand the importance of the deadline. However, if we rush, we might compromise on quality. I propose a brief extension to ensure we meet our standards. What do you think?"

3. **Objective:**
   - Address the conflict directly and professionally.
   - Show respect for their perspective while presenting your own.
   - Aim for a mutually beneficial solution.

Scenario 3: Giving Feedback to a Lion's Team Member

1. **Setup:**
   - You need to provide constructive feedback to a Lion's team member who has been dominating team meetings.
   - The goal is to encourage more balanced participation without discouraging their enthusiasm.

2. **Role-Play:**
   - **You:** "I appreciate your leadership in the meetings. Your input is valuable. However, I've noticed that others are hesitating to share their ideas. What do you think about giving everyone a chance to speak first before we dive into your points?"
   - **Team Member:** "I just want to ensure we're moving forward efficiently."

- ○ **You:** "Absolutely, and that's important. By encouraging more input, we might discover additional insights that could benefit our progress even more."

3. **Objective:**
   - ○ Provide feedback in a way that acknowledges their strengths.
   - ○ Suggest improvements that align with their goals and values.
   - ○ Maintain a positive and supportive tone.

Handling Lion's doesn't have to be daunting. By being direct, concise, and respectful of their time, you can improve your interactions and build stronger relationships. Remember, practice makes perfect! Use these tips and role-playing exercises to refine your approach and confidently engage with the Lion's in your life. Happy communicating!

Chapter 4: Meet the Parrots: The Chatty Companions

Welcome to the world of Parrot's! These individuals are the life and soul of any gathering, bringing energy, enthusiasm, and a dash of chaos. They thrive on social interactions and can often be found at the centre of any activity. This chapter will help you understand the traits of Parrot's, recognize them in real life, and learn how to connect with them effectively.

Traits and Characteristics: Energetic, Sociable, and Sometimes Overwhelming

Parrot's are the vibrant canaries of the personality spectrum. Let's break down what makes them tick:

Energetic:

- **High Energy Levels:** Parrot's are always on the go. They have a boundless supply of energy that keeps them active and engaged.
- **Enthusiastic:** They approach life with excitement and passion, often inspiring those around them.

Sociable:

- **People-Oriented:** Parrot's love being around others. They are natural networkers and enjoy meeting new people.
- **Communicative:** They are great talkers and listeners, always eager to share stories and ideas.

Sometimes Overwhelming:

- **Attention-Seeking:** Their need for social interaction can sometimes come across as attention-seeking or overly enthusiastic.
- **Disorganised:** Their high energy and spontaneous nature can make them appear disorganised or scatterbrained.

Real-Life Examples: The Life of the Party, the Charismatic Salesperson

Parrot's are easy to spot in any environment due to their outgoing and charismatic nature. Here are a few common examples:

The Life of the Party:

- **At Social Gatherings:** This person is always at the centre of the group, telling stories, making jokes, and keeping the energy high.
- **Personality Traits:** They're the ones who know everyone and make sure everyone is having a good time.

The Charismatic Salesperson:

- **In the Workplace:** This employee can sell anything to anyone. They thrive in sales and marketing roles due to their natural charm and persuasiveness.
- **Interaction Style:** They build quick rapport with clients and use their enthusiasm to close deals.

The Enthusiastic Friend:

- **In Personal Life:** This friend is always planning the next adventure or social event. They bring excitement and spontaneity to your social circle.
- **Communication Style:** They are always eager to chat, often jumping from one topic to another with infectious enthusiasm.

Worksheet: Identify the Parrot's in Your Life

Now, it's time to identify the Parrot's around you. This worksheet will help you pinpoint these energetic, sociable individuals and understand how to interact with them more effectively.

Step 1: List People You Know Think about the people in your life—friends, family, colleagues, and acquaintances. Write down the names of those who stand out as energetic and sociable.

Step 2: Evaluate Their Traits For each person on your list, consider the following questions:

- Do they have high energy levels and enthusiasm?
- Are they very sociable and enjoy being around people?
- Do they often take the spotlight in social settings?
- Can their energy sometimes be overwhelming or disorganised?

Step 3: Note Your Interactions Reflect on your interactions with these individuals:

- How do they communicate with you? (Excitedly, frequently, and often jumping between topics?)
- How do you feel when you interact with them? (Energised, overwhelmed, entertained?)
- What strategies have you used to get along with them?

Step 4: Plan Your Approach Based on your reflections, develop a strategy for interacting with the Parrot's in your life:

- **Engage Actively:** Show interest in their stories and participate in their activities.
- **Appreciate Their Energy:** Acknowledge their enthusiasm and let it inspire you.
- **Set Boundaries Kindly:** If their energy becomes overwhelming, set boundaries gently but firmly.
- **Encourage Their Ideas:** Support their spontaneous ideas and adventures, as they thrive on encouragement and positive feedback.

Example Worksheet Entry:

Person: Jake (Friend)

- **Traits:** High energy, loves social events, always planning new activities.
- **Interactions:** Excitedly discusses plans, frequently calls or texts with new ideas.
- **Plan:** Engage in conversations, show enthusiasm for his plans, set boundaries if needed by suggesting quieter activities when feeling overwhelmed.

By identifying the Parrot's in your life and understanding their traits, you can improve your interactions and build stronger, more dynamic relationships. Remember, Parrot's thrive on connection and excitement, so embrace their energy and enjoy the ride!

Chapter 5: Surviving Parrot Fever

Interacting with Parrot's can be both exhilarating and exhausting. Their infectious enthusiasm and high energy can light up a room, but knowing how to manage these interactions without getting overwhelmed is crucial. This chapter will provide you with practical communication tips, dos and don'ts, and a fun exercise to help you thrive in the company of Parrot's.

Communication Tips: Be Enthusiastic and Open

When dealing with Parrot's, matching their energy and showing genuine interest in their stories and ideas can make a world of difference. Here's how you can communicate effectively with them:

Be Enthusiastic:

- **Show Genuine Interest:** Engage actively in their conversations. Smile, nod, and respond with enthusiasm. Phrases like "That's awesome!" or "Tell me more!" show that you're genuinely interested.
- **Use Positive Language:** Keep the conversation upbeat. Use words and phrases that reflect excitement and positivity.

Be Open:

- **Listen Attentively:** Parrot's love to share their stories and ideas. Give them your full attention and avoid interrupting. Show that you're listening by asking follow-up questions and making encouraging comments.
- **Be Receptive to New Ideas:** Parrot's thrive on creativity and spontaneity. Be open to their suggestions and willing to try new things, even if they seem unconventional.

To navigate your interactions with Parrot's effectively, keep these dos and don'ts in mind:

Dos:

- **Do Engage in Their Stories:** Participate actively in their storytelling. Ask questions, share your thoughts, and show that you're interested.
- **Do Appreciate Their Enthusiasm:** Acknowledge and appreciate their energy and excitement. Let them know that their positivity is contagious.
- **Do Encourage Their Ideas:** Support their creative ideas and plans. Even if you have reservations, express them tactfully and focus on the positives first.

Don'ts:

- **Don't Dampen Their Enthusiasm:** Avoid being overly critical or dismissive of their ideas. Phrases like "That won't work" or "That's a bad idea" can deflate their spirit.
- **Don't Ignore Their Input:** Make sure to acknowledge their contributions. Ignoring their ideas or not giving them a chance to speak can make them feel undervalued.
- **Don't Overwhelm Them with Details:** Parrot's can become easily bored with too much information. Keep your explanations concise and focus on the big picture.

Fun Exercise: Plan an Event with a Parrot's

Planning an event with a Parrot's can be a fantastic way to harness their enthusiasm and creativity while practising your communication skills. Follow these steps for a fun and collaborative experience:

Step 1: Choose an Event Decide on the type of event you want to plan. It could be a party, a group outing, a creative project, or even a spontaneous adventure.

Step 2: Brainstorm Ideas Sit down with your Parrot's friend or colleague and brainstorm ideas for the event. Encourage them to share their wildest and most creative suggestions. Use phrases like:

- "What do you think would make this event unforgettable?"
- "I'd love to hear your ideas on how we can make this fun."

Step 3: Assign Roles Identify each person's strengths and assign roles accordingly. Parrot's are great at coming up with creative ideas and engaging people, so give them tasks that align with these strengths. For example:

- **Parrot's :** Planning the theme, sending out invitations, coming up with games or activities.
- **You:** Handling logistics, making detailed plans, managing the budget.

Step 4: Plan the Details Work together to plan the finer details of the event. Keep the conversation dynamic and exciting. Use bullet points or a checklist to keep track of the main points, but avoid overwhelming them with too much information at once.

Step 5: Execute the Plan On the day of the event, let your Parrot's partner take the lead in energising the crowd and ensuring everyone is having a great time. Support them by handling any behind-the-scenes tasks and ensuring everything runs smoothly.

Example Event Plan:

Event: Summer Beach Party

Brainstorming Session:

- **Parrot's :** "Let's have a beach volleyball tournament, a sandcastle-building contest, and a tropical drink station!"
- **You:** "Great ideas! How about we also set up a barbecue area and some chill-out zones with beach umbrellas and lounge chairs?"

Roles:

- **Parrot's :** Invite friends, plan activities, and handle the drink station.
- **You:** Book the beach location, organise food and drinks, and manage the budget.

Planning the Details:

- **Parrot's :** "I'll create a fun invitation and send it out. I'll also bring the volleyball net and prizes for the contests."
- **You:** "I'll handle the catering and make sure we have enough chairs and umbrellas. Let's make a checklist to ensure we don't miss anything."

Executing the Plan:

- **Parrot's :** "Hey everyone! Welcome to the beach party! Who's ready for some volleyball?"
- **You:** (Quietly managing the food setup, ensuring everyone has what they need.)

By collaborating with a Parrot's on an event, you'll experience firsthand how their enthusiasm can elevate any occasion. You'll also learn to balance their creativity with practical planning, making for a successful and enjoyable partnership.

Surviving Parrot's Fever means embracing their energy, engaging with their ideas, and balancing their spontaneity with practical planning. With these communication tips, dos and don'ts, and the fun exercise of planning an event together, you'll be well-equipped to thrive in the lively company of Parrot's. Enjoy the excitement they bring and let their enthusiasm inspire you!

Chapter 6: Meet the Dolphins: The Calm Navigators

Welcome to the serene world of the Dolphins! These individuals are the calm, steady anchors in the whirlwind of personalities. They bring patience, reliability, and a sense of stability to any group. This chapter will help you understand the traits of Dolphins, recognize them in real life, and learn how to connect with them effectively.

Traits and Characteristics: Patient, Reliable, and Sometimes Resistant to Change

Dolphins are the peaceful koalas of the personality spectrum. Let's dive into what makes them unique:

Patient:

- **Calm Under Pressure:** Dolphins are known for their calm demeanour, even in stressful situations. They rarely get flustered and approach problems with a level-headed attitude.
- **Good Listeners:** They have the patience to listen attentively and empathetically, making others feel heard and valued.

Reliable:

- **Dependable:** You can always count on a Dolphin. They are consistent in their actions and follow through on commitments.
- **Loyal:** Dolphins are steadfastly loyal to their friends, family, and colleagues. They value long-term relationships and are always there when you need them.

Sometimes Resistant to Change:

- **Preference for Stability:** Dolphins prefer routines and familiar environments. They find comfort in predictability and may be hesitant to embrace change.

- **Cautious:** They take their time to assess situations before making decisions. This cautious nature can sometimes be perceived as resistance to change.

Real-Life Examples: The Dependable Friend, the Nurturing Parent

Dolphins are often the unsung heroes in our lives. Here are a few common examples:

The Dependable Friend:

- **In Social Settings:** This friend is always there for you, whether you need a shoulder to cry on or someone to help you move. They are the glue that holds the group together.
- **Personality Traits:** They are reliable, supportive, and always willing to lend a hand.

The Nurturing Parent:

- **At Home:** This parent creates a stable, loving environment for their children. They provide consistency and security, making their home a safe haven.
- **Interaction Style:** They are patient and attentive, always putting their family's needs first.

The Steady Colleague:

- **In the Workplace:** This colleague can be relied upon to get the job done without fuss. They are methodical and consistent, providing a steady presence in the office.
- **Work Style:** They prefer clear guidelines and established procedures, and they work diligently to maintain high standards.

Now, it's time to identify the Dolphins around you. This worksheet will help you pinpoint these patient, reliable individuals and understand how to interact with them more effectively.

Step 1: List People You Know Think about the people in your life—friends, family, colleagues, and acquaintances. Write down the names of those who stand out as patient and reliable.

Step 2: Evaluate Their Traits For each person on your list, consider the following questions:

- Do they remain calm under pressure?
- Are they good listeners who make others feel heard?
- Can you always rely on them to follow through on commitments?
- Do they prefer stability and routine, sometimes resisting change?

Step 3: Note Your Interactions Reflect on your interactions with these individuals:

- How do they communicate with you? (Patiently, attentively, and calmly?)
- How do you feel when you interact with them? (Comforted, supported, secure?)
- What strategies have you used to get along with them?

Step 4: Plan Your Approach Based on your reflections, develop a strategy for interacting with the Dolphins in your life:

- **Be Patient:** Allow them time to process information and make decisions.
- **Show Appreciation:** Acknowledge their reliability and support. Let them know their efforts are valued.
- **Provide Stability:** When possible, offer consistency and predictability in your interactions. Avoid sudden changes or surprises.
- **Encourage Gently:** If you need them to embrace change, do so gently and with clear explanations of the benefits.

Example Worksheet Entry:

Person: Emma (Colleague)

- **Traits:** Calm under pressure, reliable, prefers routine.
- **Interactions:** Patiently listens during meetings, consistently meets deadlines, prefers established procedures.
- **Plan:** Provide clear, detailed information for tasks, show appreciation for her reliability, introduce changes gradually with thorough explanations.

By identifying the Dolphins in your life and understanding their traits, you can improve your interactions and build stronger, more supportive relationships. Remember, Dolphins thrive on stability and reliability, so appreciate their calm presence and let them know how much you value their steadfast support.

Chapter 7: Navigating with Dolphins

Interacting with Dolphins can be incredibly rewarding due to their calm, reliable nature. However, to get the best out of these interactions, you need to approach them with patience and support. This chapter will provide you with practical communication tips, dos and don'ts, and a fun exercise to help you strengthen your connections with Dolphins.

Communication Tips: Be Patient and Supportive

When dealing with Dolphins, patience and support are key. Here's how you can effectively communicate with them:

Be Patient:

- **Give Them Time:** Dolphins need time to process information and make decisions. Avoid rushing them. For example, if you need a decision from them, provide the information well in advance and follow up gently if necessary.
- **Listen Attentively:** Show that you value their thoughts and feelings by listening without interrupting. Dolphins appreciate being heard and understood.

Be Supportive:

- **Offer Encouragement:** Recognize their efforts and achievements. Simple acknowledgements like "I really appreciate your hard work" or "Thank you for always being reliable" can go a long way.
- **Provide Reassurance:** Dolphins can be hesitant about change. Reassure them by explaining the reasons behind changes and highlighting the benefits.

To navigate your interactions with Dolphins effectively, keep these dos and don'ts in mind:

Dos:

- **Do Show Appreciation for Their Reliability:** Acknowledge and thank them for their dependable nature. Dolphins take pride in being reliable and appreciate recognition.
- **Do Create a Calm Environment:** Dolphins thrive in stable, low-stress environments. Maintain a calm demeanour and avoid unnecessary conflict.
- **Do Be Consistent:** Dolphins appreciate routine and predictability. Try to be consistent in your actions and promises.

Don'ts:

- **Don't Pressure Them for Quick Decisions:** Dolphins need time to think things through. Pressuring them can cause stress and lead to hasty decisions that they may regret later.
- **Don't Overwhelm Them with Change:** Introduce changes gradually and provide clear explanations. Sudden changes can make Dolphins feel unsettled.
- **Don't Dismiss Their Concerns:** If a Dolphin expresses concerns or hesitations, take them seriously. Dismissing their feelings can damage trust and communication.

Fun Exercise: Meditative Activities with a Dolphin

Engaging in calming, meditative activities with a Dolphin can help strengthen your bond and provide a relaxing environment for both of you. Here are some activities you can try:

Step 1: Choose a Meditative Activity Select an activity that promotes relaxation and calmness. Some examples include:

- **Yoga:** A gentle yoga session can help Reduce stress and promote mindfulness.

- **Nature Walks:** Taking a walk in a peaceful natural setting can be incredibly soothing.
- **Meditation:** Practising meditation together can enhance relaxation and mental clarity.
- **Gardening:** Tending to plants can be a therapeutic and rewarding activity.

Step 2: Set the Scene Create a calm and serene environment for your chosen activity. Ensure the space is quiet, free from distractions, and comfortable.

Step 3: Participate Together Engage in the activity together, focusing on the present moment. Encourage each other to relax and enjoy the experience. Here are some ways to enhance the activity:

- **Yoga:** Follow a guided session or gentle flow that emphasises deep breathing and relaxation. Offer words of encouragement and support.
- **Nature Walks:** Walk at a leisurely pace, taking in the sights and sounds of nature. Point out interesting plants, birds, or landscapes.
- **Meditation:** Choose a guided meditation or simply sit in silence together, focusing on your breath. Share your experiences afterward.
- **Gardening:** Work on a gardening project together, such as planting flowers or tending to a vegetable patch. Enjoy the satisfaction of nurturing plants.

Example Activity: Yoga Session

Setup:

- **Choose a Quiet Space:** Find a quiet room or an outdoor spot where you won't be disturbed.
- **Gather Supplies:** Have yoga mats, comfortable clothing, and perhaps some soothing music or essential oils.

Activity:

- **Start with Deep Breathing:** Begin with a few minutes of deep breathing to centre yourselves.
- **Follow a Gentle Flow:** Guide each other through a series of gentle yoga poses, focusing on relaxation and mindfulness.
- **End with Meditation:** Finish with a short meditation or savasana (resting pose), allowing your bodies and minds to fully relax.

Reflection:

- **Share Your Experience:** After the session, take a few moments to share how you felt during the practice. Discuss any thoughts or feelings that arose.

By engaging in meditative activities with a Dolphin, you create a shared space of calm and connection. These activities not only strengthen your bond but also provide a rejuvenating experience for both of you.

Dolphining your interactions means embracing patience, offering support, and creating a calm environment for your Dolphin friends and colleagues. With these communication tips, dos and don'ts, and the fun exercise of meditative activities, you'll be well-equipped to build stronger, more supportive relationships with the Dolphins in your life. Appreciate their reliability and let their calm presence bring balance to your interactions.

Chapter 8: Meet the Owls: The Wise Analysts

Welcome to the meticulous world of the Owls! These individuals are the analytical owls of the personality spectrum, known for their attention to detail, logical thinking, and sometimes nitpicky tendencies. This chapter will help you understand the traits of Owls, recognize them in real life, and learn how to connect with them effectively.

Traits and Characteristics: Detail-Oriented, Logical, and Sometimes Nitpicky

Owls are the methodical and precise owls of the personality spectrum. Let's dive into what makes them unique:

Detail-Oriented:

- **Meticulous:** Owls have a keen eye for detail and a strong focus on accuracy. They take pride in their ability to spot errors and ensure everything is perfect.
- **Thorough:** They leave no stone unturned in their quest for completeness. Whether it's a report, a project, or a plan, Owls ensure every detail is coveLion's.

Logical:

- **Analytical Thinkers:** Owls approach problems and situations logically and methodically. They rely on data and facts to make decisions and often excel in roles that require critical thinking.
- **Rational:** Emotions take a backseat to logic and reason for Owls. They value objective analysis and clear, rational thought.

Sometimes Nitpicky:

- **Perfectionists:** Their high standards can sometimes come across as nitpicky or overly critical. They have a low tolerance for mistakes and may focus on minor details others might overlook.

- **Cautious:** Owls prefer to take their time to ensure everything is done correctly, which can sometimes lead to delays or a perceived lack of flexibility.

Owls play crucial roles in various aspects of life and work. Here are a few common examples:

The Meticulous Accountant:

- **In the Workplace:** This person ensures that financial records are accurate and compliant with regulations. They are the backbone of any finance team.
- **Personality Traits:** They are detail-oriented, precise, and highly organised.

The Critical Thinker:

- **In Academic Settings:** This student or professor excels in analysing complex theories and concepts. They thrive in environments that require deep thinking and critical analysis.
- **Interaction Style:** They ask probing questions and seek to understand the underlying principles of any topic.

The Quality Control Specialist:

- **In Manufacturing or Tech:** This person ensures products meet the highest standards of quality. They meticulously check every detail to prevent errors and defects.
- **Work Style:** They are methodical, patient, and have a sharp eye for detail.

Worksheet: Identify the Owls in Your Life

Now, it's time to identify the Owls around you. This worksheet will help you pinpoint these detail-oriented, logical individuals and understand how to interact with them more effectively.

Step 1: List People You Know Think about the people in your life—friends, family, colleagues, and acquaintances. Write down the names of those who stand out as detail-oriented and logical.

Step 2: Evaluate Their Traits For each person on your list, consider the following questions:

- Do they have a keen eye for detail and accuracy?
- Are they methodical and thorough in their approach?
- Do they rely on data and facts to make decisions?
- Can they sometimes be perceived as nitpicky or overly critical?

Step 3: Note Your Interactions Reflect on your interactions with these individuals:

- How do they communicate with you? (Logically, with a focus on details?)
- How do you feel when you interact with them? (Informed, challenged, sometimes scrutinised?)
- What strategies have you used to get along with them?

Step 4: Plan Your Approach Based on your reflections, develop a strategy for interacting with the Owls in your life:

- **Provide Details:** When communicating with Owls, provide detailed and accurate information. Avoid vague statements and be prepared to back up your points with data.
- **Be Logical:** Structure your arguments logically and focus on facts. Owls appreciate clear, rational thought.
- **Show Respect for Their Standards:** Acknowledge their high standards and attention to detail. Show that you value their meticulous approach.

Example Worksheet Entry:

Person: Alex (Colleague)

- **Traits:** Detail-oriented, analytical, prefers data-driven decisions.
- **Interactions:** Often asks for detailed explanations, prefers thorough reports, focuses on accuracy.
- **Plan:** Provide comprehensive data and detailed reports, present information logically, respect their need for thoroughness.

By identifying the Owls in your life and understanding their traits, you can improve your interactions and build stronger, more respectful relationships. Remember, Owls thrive on detail and logic, so appreciate their analytical nature and let their precision enhance your interactions.

Chapter 9: Learning from the Owls

Engaging effectively with Owls requires a clear, precise approach that respects their need for detail and logical analysis. This chapter will provide you with communication tips, dos and don'ts, and a fun exercise to help you navigate your interactions with Owls smoothly and effectively.

Communication Tips: Be Clear and Precise

When dealing with Owls, clarity and precision are paramount. Here's how you can communicate effectively with them:

Be Clear:

- **Use Specific Language:** Avoid vague or ambiguous statements. Be specific and to the point in your communication. For example, instead of saying "We need to improve sales," say "We need to increase sales by 15% over the next quarter."
- **Clarify Expectations:** Make sure expectations are clearly defined. Outline what needs to be done, by whom, and by when.

Be Precise:

- **Provide Detailed Information:** Owls appreciate comprehensive and accurate information. Include all relevant details and data to support your points. For instance, if presenting a report, ensure it is thorough and well-documented.
- **Organise Your Thoughts:** Structure your communication logically. Use bullet points, headings, and subheadings to make your points clear and easy to follow.

To navigate your interactions with Owls effectively, keep these dos and don'ts in mind:

Dos:

- **Do Provide Detailed Information:** When discussing a topic with an Owl, ensure you have all the facts and figures ready. They value data and evidence-based discussions.
- **Do Answer Their Questions:** Owls are naturally inquisitive and will ask many questions to understand the details. Take the time to answer their questions thoroughly.
- **Do Be Logical:** Present your arguments and ideas in a logical sequence. Use cause-and-effect reasoning and back up your statements with solid evidence.

Don'ts:

- **Don't Overlook Their Questions:** Ignoring or dismissing their questions can frustrate Owls and make them feel undervalued. Always address their queries seriously.
- **Don't Rush Decisions:** Owls need time to analyse and consider all the details before making decisions. Avoid pushing them for quick answers.
- **Don't Be Vague:** Ambiguity can be unsettling for Owls. Avoid generalisations and unclear statements.

Fun Exercise: Problem-Solving Tasks with a Owl

Engaging in problem-solving tasks with an Owl can be an excellent way to harness their analytical skills while fostering teamwork. Here's a structured exercise to help you collaborate effectively:

Step 1: Choose a Problem-Solving Task Select a task that requires detailed analysis and logical thinking. Some examples include:

- **Data Analysis:** Analysing sales data to identify trends and make projections.
- **Project Planning:** Creating a detailed project plan, including timelines, resources, and risk assessments.
- **Puzzle Solving:** Working together on complex puzzles or brain teasers that require careful thought and precision.

Step 2: Gather Necessary Information Ensure you have all the necessary information and tools for the task. For instance, if you're analysing data, gather all relevant datasets and analysis tools.

Step 3: Plan Your Approach Discuss and agree on a structuLion's approach to tackle the task. Break down the problem into smaller, manageable parts and assign roles based on strengths. For example:

- **Identify the Problem:** Clearly define the problem you need to solve.
- **Gather Data:** Collect all relevant information and data points.
- **Analyse:** Examine the data methodically, looking for patterns and insights.
- **Develop Solutions:** Brainstorm potential solutions based on your analysis.
- **Evaluate and Decide:** Assess the feasibility of each solution and decide on the best course of action.

Step 4: Work Collaboratively Engage in the task together, following the agreed plan. Communicate regularly to share insights and progress. Use the following strategies:

- **Ask Questions:** Encourage Owls to ask questions and probe deeper into the details.
- **Share Findings:** Regularly update each other on your findings and analysis.
- **Stay Focused:** Keep the discussion focused on the task at hand, avoiding distractions.

Step 5: Review and Reflect Once you've completed the task, review the process and results together. Discuss what worked well and any challenges you encountered. Reflect on how you can improve your collaboration in the future.

Example Activity: Data Analysis Task

Task: Analyse the sales data from the past year to identify trends and make projections for the next quarter.

Setup:

- **Gather Data:** Collect all relevant sales data, including monthly sales figures, product performance, and market conditions.
- **Choose Tools:** Select analysis tools such as spreadsheets, data visualisation software, and statistical methods.

Activity:

- **Identify the Problem:** Define the goal—e.g., "We need to identify key sales trends and project future performance."
- **Gather Data:** Collect and organise the sales data.
- **Analyse:** Examine the data to identify patterns and trends. Use charts and graphs to visualise the findings.
- **Develop Solutions:** Based on the analysis, brainstorm strategies to improve sales.
- **Evaluate and Decide:** Assess the feasibility of each strategy and decide on the best approach.

Reflection:

- **Review Findings:** Discuss the insights gained from the analysis.
- **Evaluate Process:** Reflect on the collaboration process—what worked well and what could be improved.
- **Plan Next Steps:** Outline the next steps based on the decisions made.

By engaging in problem-solving tasks with an Owl, you can leverage their analytical strengths while improving your collaborative skills. This exercise not only enhances your ability to work together but also demonstrates the value of their detailed, logical approach.

Singing the Owls without losing the tune means communicating with clarity and precision, respecting their need for detailed information, and addressing their questions thoroughly. With these communication tips, dos and don'ts, and the fun exercise of problem-solving tasks, you'll be well-equipped to build stronger, more productive relationships with the Owls in your life. Appreciate their analytical nature and let their precision and logic enhance your interactions.

Chapter 10: Mixing Animals: Blending Different Personalities

In the Animal world of personalities, understanding how different types interact can lead to more harmonious relationships, whether in the workplace, at home, or in social settings. This chapter explores the dynamics of blending different personality types, provides real-life examples, and includes a worksheet to help you map out the personality blend in your social circle.

Understanding Combinations: How Different Types Interact

Each personality type brings its unique strengths and challenges to interactions. Here's a look at how different combinations can play out:

Lion's (Dominant) and Parrot's (Influential):

- **Interaction:** Dynamic and energetic. Lion's bring determination and decisiveness, while Parrot's add creativity and enthusiasm.
- **Strengths:** Together, they can drive projects forward with both efficiency and innovative flair.
- **Challenges:** Potential for conflict if the Lion's need for control clashes with the Parrot's 's desire for spontaneity.

Lion's (Dominant) and Dolphin (Stable):

- **Interaction:** Productive and balanced. Lion's push for results, and Dolphins provide stability and support.
- **Strengths:** Dolphins can temper the Lion's intensity, while Lion's can motivate Dolphins to take action.
- **Challenges:** Dolphins may feel overwhelmed by the Lion's assertiveness, while Lion's might get frustrated with the Dolphin's slower pace.

Lion's (Dominant) and Owl (Conscientious):

- **Interaction:** Goal-oriented and thorough. Lion'sF focus on achieving objectives, and Owls ensure precision and quality.
- **Strengths:** Together, they can achieve high standards and ambitious goals.
- **Challenges:** Lion's may find Owls too nitpicky, while Owls might see Lion's as too impulsive.

Parrot's (Influential) and Dolphin (Stable):

- **Interaction:** Harmonious and friendly. Parrot's bring excitement and energy, while Dolphins offer patience and consistency.
- **Strengths:** Dolphins can provide a calming influence on Parrot's, and Parrot's can encourage Dolphins to be more outgoing.
- **Challenges:** Dolphins might find Parrot's' energy overwhelming, while Parrot's might get bored with Dolphins' preference for routine.

Parrot's (Influential) and Owl (Conscientious):

- **Interaction:** Creative and analytical. Parrot's generate ideas, and Owls refine them with careful analysis.
- **Strengths:** This combination can lead to innovative yet well-thought-out solutions.
- **Challenges:** Owls may see Parrot's as too scattered, while Parrot's might view Owls as overly critical.

Dolphin (Stable) and Owl (Conscientious):

- **Interaction:** Steady and systematic. Dolphins offer reliability, and Owls bring precision and thoroughness.
- **Strengths:** Together, they can create a stable, efficient, and high-quality work environment.
- **Challenges:** Dolphins might find Owls too rigid, while Owls might see Dolphins as too slow or passive.

Real-Life Examples: Office Dynamics, Family Gatherings

Example 1: The Marketing Team

- **Lion's (Project Leaders):** Drive the team towards meeting deadlines and achieving targets.
- **Parrot's (Creative Directors):** Infuse campaigns with innovative ideas and enthusiasm.
- **Dolphins (Support Staff):** Provide dependable support and ensure tasks are completed smoothly.
- **Owls (Analysts):** Ensure the accuracy of data and fine-tune campaign details.

Dynamic:

- The Lion's leaders set ambitious goals.
- The Parrot's brainstorm creative strategies.
- The Dolphins manage the day-to-day operations.
- The Owls analyse market data to refine campaigns.

Challenges:

- Balancing the Lion's urgency with the Dolphin's need for stability.
- Integrating the Parrot's 's creativity with the Owl's demand for precision.

Example 2: The IT Department

- **Lion's (Managers):** Push for swift implementation of new technologies.
- **Parrot's (Developers):** Bring innovative solutions and ideas.
- **Dolphins (Support Technicians):** Ensure the smooth operation of systems.
- **Owls (Quality Assurance):** Meticulously test and debug software.

Dynamic:

- The Lion's managers drive technological advancement.
- The Parrot's develop creative software solutions.
- The Dolphins maintain system stability.
- The Owls ensure the highest quality and functionality of the products.

Challenges:

- The Lion's impatience for quick results versus the Owl's need for thorough testing.
- The Parrot's 's preference for creative freedom versus the Dolphin's desire for consistency.

Family Gatherings:

Example 1: The Smith Family Reunion

- **Lion's (Uncle John):** Organises and leads activities, ensuring everything runs smoothly.
- **Parrot's (Cousin Amy):** Keeps the atmosphere lively and engages everyone in fun games.
- **Dolphins (Aunt Mary):** Makes sure everyone is comfortable and well-fed.
- **Owls (Grandpa Joe):** Documents the event with detailed notes and photographs.

Dynamic:

- Uncle John takes charge of the event planning.
- Cousin Amy entertains with her vibrant personality.
- Aunt Mary provides steady support and hospitality.
- Grandpa Joe captures every moment with precision.

Challenges:

- Balancing Uncle John's structured activities with Cousin Amy's spontaneous games.
- Ensuring Aunt Mary's efforts are appreciated without overwhelming her with tasks.

Example 2: The Jones Family Dinner

- **Lion's (Dad):** Leads the conversation and makes decisions about dinner plans.
- **Parrot's (Teenage Daughter):** Brings excitement with her stories and jokes.
- **Dolphins (Mom):** Ensures everyone's needs are met and maintains a peaceful environment.
- **Owls (Son):** Organises the dinner setup and makes sure everything is perfect.

Dynamic:

- Dad directs the evening's schedule.
- The daughter keeps everyone entertained.
- Mom provides a calming presence and support.
- The son ensures every detail of the dinner is meticulously arranged.

Challenges:

- Managing Dad's authoritative style with the son's need for thorough preparation.
- Harmonising the daughter's lively energy with Mom's desire for a tranquil evening.

Worksheet: Map Out Your Social Circle's Personality Blend

This worksheet will help you identify and understand the personality blend in your social circle. By mapping out the different personalities, you can better appreciate the dynamics at play and foster more harmonious interactions.

Step 1: List People in Your Social Circle Think about your family, friends, colleagues, and acquaintances. Write down the names of those who are part of your regular interactions.

Step 2: Identify Their Personality Types For each person, determine their primary personality type based on the descriptions provided in earlier chapters. Use the following abbreviations for simplicity:

- **R:** Lion's (Dominant)
- **Y:** Parrot's (Influential)
- **G:** Dolphin (Stable)
- **B:** Owl (Conscientious)

Step 3: Map Out Interactions Create a chart or diagram that maps out the interactions between different personality types in your social circle. Consider the following:

- **Who interacts with whom most frequently?**
- **What are the common dynamics and challenges in these interactions?**
- **How can you use the strengths of each personality type to improve these interactions?**

Example Worksheet Entry:

Name	Personality Type	Common Interactions	Challenges	Strategies for Improvement
Sarah	Y	Social events, brainstorming sessions	Overwhelms with enthusiasm	Encourage her creativity, set some structure
Orion	R	Team meetings, decision-making processes	Pushes for quick decisions	Provide data to support decisions, ask for input
Emily	G	One-on-one discussions, project support	Hesitant to change	Reassure with clear explanations, give time
Mike	B	Detailed project work, quality checks	Focuses on minor details	Acknowledge his thoroughness, balance with bigger picture

Reflection Questions:

1. What patterns do you notice in your social circle's personality blend?

2. Which interactions are most harmonious, and why?

3. Which interactions are most challenging, and how can they be improved?

By completing this worksheet, you can gain a clearer understanding of the personality dynamics in your social circle. This knowledge will help you foster more effective and harmonious relationships by leveraging the strengths of each personality type and addressing potential challenges constructively.

Mixing animals and blending different personalities can create a rich tapestry of interactions that enrich our lives. By understanding how different personality types interact, recognizing real-life examples, and mapping out your social circle's personality blend, you can navigate these interactions with greater ease and effectiveness. Embrace the diversity of personalities around you and use this knowledge to build stronger, more harmonious relationships.

Chapter 11: Conflict Resolution in the Animal Kingdom

Navigating conflicts among different personality types can feel like manoeuvring through a dense jungle. Understanding the common conflicts and learning effective resolution strategies can help you foster a more harmonious environment. This chapter delves into typical clashes between personality types, offers practical strategies for resolution, and includes a worksheet to analyse and resolve recent conflicts.

Common Conflicts: Lion's vs. Owls, Parrot's vs. Dolphins

Different personality types have distinct ways of perceiving and interacting with the world, which can sometimes lead to conflicts. Here are some common conflicts and their underlying reasons:

Lion's (Dominant) vs. Owls (Conscientious):

- **Conflict Source:** Lion's are action-oriented and seek quick results, while Owls are detail-oriented and prefer thorough analysis.
- **Typical Scenario:** A Lion's might push for immediate implementation of a new project, while an Owl insists on comprehensive research and planning first.
- **Underlying Tension:** Lion's may see Owls as overly cautious and slow, while Owls may view Lion's as impulsive and reckless.

Parrot's (Influential) vs. Dolphins (Stable):

- **Conflict Source:** Parrot's are enthusiastic and spontaneous, whereas Dolphins value stability and routine.
- **Typical Scenario:** A Parrot's might propose a last-minute change to plans for the sake of excitement, while a Dolphin prefers sticking to the established schedule.
- **Underlying Tension:** Parrot's might perceive Dolphins as resistant to change and boring, while Dolphins might find Parrot's chaotic and unpredictable.

Resolving conflicts between different personality types requires understanding, patience, and effective communication. Here are some strategies:

Compromise:

- **Find Common Ground:** Identify shared goals and values that both parties agree on. For example, both Lions and Owls want the project to succeed, even if they have different approaches.
- **Mutual Adjustments:** Encourage both parties to make small adjustments to accommodate each other's preferences. For example, a Lion's could agree to a shorter planning phase if the Owl provides a concise analysis.

Communication Techniques:

- **Active Listening:** Encourage each party to actively listen to the other's perspective without interrupting. This helps in understanding the underlying concerns and motivations.
- **Empathy:** Foster empathy by asking each party to consider how the other person feels and why they hold their position. For instance, Lion's can recognize that Owls' caution stems from a desire for quality and accuracy.
- **Clear and Direct Communication:** Use clear and direct language to express needs and concerns. For example, a Parrot's can explicitly state the need for flexibility, while a Dolphin can clearly outline their need for stability.

Specific Techniques:

- **Mediation:** Involve a neutral third party to facilitate discussions and help find a resolution that satisfies both parties.
- **Structured Dialogue:** Set up a structured dialogue where each party takes turns speaking and listening, ensuring that both sides are heard.

- **Problem-Solving Approach:** Focus on finding solutions rather than assigning blame. Encourage brainstorming sessions to come up with mutually beneficial resolutions.

Worksheet: Analyse a Recent Conflict and Apply Resolution Strategies

Use this worksheet to analyse a recent conflict involving different personality types and apply the resolution strategies discussed.

Step 1: Describe the Conflict

- **Parties Involved:** Identify the individuals and their personality types.
- **Conflict Description:** Provide a brief overview of the conflict, including the main issue and any key events.

Example Entry:

- **Parties Involved:** John (Lion's), Emily (Owl)
- **Conflict Description:** John wanted to launch a new marketing campaign immediately, while Emily insisted on conducting a detailed market analysis first. Tensions rose as John saw Emily's caution as a delay tactic, and Emily viewed John's urgency as reckless.

Step 2: Identify the Underlying Tensions

- **Lion's Perspective:** What are the Lion's primary concerns and motivations?
- **Owl's Perspective:** What are the Owl's primary concerns and motivations?

Example Entry:

- **Lion's Perspective:** John is focused on achieving quick results to stay ahead of competitors.
- **Owl's Perspective:** Emily is concerned about the campaign's effectiveness and wants to ensure it is well-researched and error-free.

Step 3: Apply Resolution Strategies

- **Compromise Solution:** What common ground can be found? What mutual adjustments can be made?
- **Communication Techniques Used:** How can active listening, empathy, and clear communication be applied?

Example Entry:

- **Compromise Solution:** John agrees to a shorter analysis period if Emily provides a summary of key insights rather than a full report.
- **Communication Techniques Used:** During a mediated meeting, both John and Emily practise active listening, acknowledging each other's concerns. They use clear language to express their needs and agree on a revised timeline.

Step 4: Reflect on the Outcome

- **Resolution Effectiveness:** Was the conflict resolved satisfactorily? What was the outcome?
- **Lessons Learned:** What did you learn from this conflict resolution process?

Example Entry:

- **Resolution Effectiveness:** The conflict was resolved, and the campaign launched with a brief but effective analysis. Both parties felt their concerns were addressed.
- **Lessons Learned:** The importance of balancing urgency with thoroughness and the value of clear, empathetic communication.

Worksheet Template:

Step	Description	Example Entry
Parties Involved	Identify individuals and their personality types	John (Lion's), Emily (Owl)
Conflict Description	Brief overview of the conflict, main issue, key events	John wanted immediate launch; Emily wanted detailed analysis
Lion's Perspective	Lion's primary concerns and motivations	Focused on quick results
Owl's Perspective	Owl's primary concerns and motivations	Concerned about effectiveness and thoroughness
Compromise Solution	Common ground and mutual adjustments	Shorter analysis period, summary of key insights
Communication Techniques Used	Active listening, empathy, clear communication	Mediated meeting, practised active listening and clear language
Resolution Effectiveness	Was the conflict resolved satisfactorily? Outcome	Conflict resolved, campaign launched with brief analysis
Lessons Learned	What did you learn from this conflict resolution process?	Importance of balancing urgency and thoroughness, clear communication

By analysing a recent conflict and applying these resolution strategies, you can improve your ability to navigate and resolve conflicts between different personality types. This approach not only helps in resolving the immediate issue but also strengthens relationships and fosters a more collaborative environment.

Conflict resolution in the jungle of personalities requires understanding, patience, and effective communication. By recognizing common conflicts, applying practical resolution strategies, and using the provided worksheet, you can navigate conflicts more effectively and build stronger, more harmonious relationships. Embrace the diversity of personalities around you and use these tools to turn conflicts into opportunities for growth and understanding.

Chapter 12: Teamwork Makes the Dream Work

Effective teamwork harnesses the diverse strengths of individual personalities to achieve collective success. This chapter explores strategies for building effective teams, showcases real-life examples of successful teams, and provides a worksheet to help you design your ideal team.

Building Effective Teams: Utilising Different Strengths

Successful teams leverage the unique strengths and skills of each team member. Here's how to create a cohesive and productive team:

Identify and Utilise Strengths:

- **Lion's (Dominant):** Assign leadership roles where decisiveness and direction are crucial.
- **Parrot's (Influential):** Utilise their creativity and enthusiasm for brainstorming and motivating the team.
- **Dolphin (Stable):** Allocate roles that require reliability, consistency, and attention to detail.
- **Owl (Conscientious):** Entrust them with tasks that demand precision, analysis, and adherence to standards.

Foster Collaboration:

- **Open Communication:** Encourage team members to communicate openly and respectfully.
- **Clear Goals:** Define clear objectives and ensure everyone understands their role in achieving them.
- **Flexibility:** Be open to different working styles and adapt to accommodate the needs and preferences of team members.

Promote Team Spirit:

- **Celebrate Success:** Recognize and celebrate achievements to boost morale and foster a positive team culture.
- **Resolve Conflicts:** Address conflicts promptly and constructively to maintain harmony within the team.
- **Continuous Improvement:** Encourage feedback and continuous learning to enhance team performance over time.

Real-Life Examples: Successful Project Teams, Sports Teams

Successful Project Teams:

Example 1: Technology Development Team

- **Composition:**
    - **Lion's (Dominant):** Project Manager who sets goals and drives the team towards milestones.
    - **Parrot's (Influential):** Creative Designer who brings innovative ideas and motivates the team.
    - **Dolphin (Stable):** Quality Assurance Specialist who ensures the product meets high standards.
    - **Owl (Conscientious):** Data Analyst who provides detailed insights for informed decision-making.

Dynamic:

- The Lion's sets the project timeline and milestones.
- The Parrot's designs intuitive user interfaces and inspires creativity.
- The Dolphin ensures product stability and reliability.
- The Owl analyses user data to refine and optimise the product.

Success Factors:

- Effective communication and collaboration.
- Leveraging individual strengths for a cohesive team effort.
- Adapting to challenges and refining strategies based on data analysis.

Example 2: Marketing Campaign Team

- **Composition:**
  - **Lion's (Dominant):** Campaign Manager who oversees strategy execution.
  - **Parrot's (Influential):** Content Creator who generates engaging marketing materials.
  - **Dolphin (Stable):** Event Coordinator who organises successful promotional events.
  - **Owl (Conscientious):** Market Researcher who provides data-driven insights.

Dynamic:

- The Lion's leads campaign planning and execution.
- The Parrot's creates compelling content to attract and retain customers.
- The Dolphin organises events that enhance brand visibility and engagement.
- The Owl conducts market research to identify target demographics and trends.

Success Factors:

- Aligning marketing strategies with market research findings.
- Engaging customers through creative and informative content.
- Collaborating effectively to execute cohesive marketing campaigns.

Sports Teams:

Example 1: Soccer Team

- **Composition:**
  - **Lion's (Dominant):** Team Captain who leads on-field strategies and decisions.
  - **Parrot's (Influential):** Forward who energises the team with goal-scoring opportunities.
  - **Dolphin (Stable):** Defender who provides a solid defensive line and stability.

   - ○ **Owl (Conscientious):** Goalkeeper who analyses opponent strategies and makes critical saves.

Dynamic:

- The Lion's lead tactical discussions and motivate the team during matches.
- The Parrot utilises creativity and agility to create scoring opportunities.
- The Dolphin maintains defensive stability and supports team coordination.
- The Owl analyses opponents' patterns to anticipate and block scoring attempts.

Success Factors:

- Effective teamwork and communication on the field.
- Leveraging individual strengths to enhance overall team performance.
- Adapting strategies based on opponent analysis and game dynamics.

Worksheet: Design Your Ideal Team

Use this worksheet to design your ideal team by considering the roles and strengths of each personality type.

Step 1: Define Team Objectives

- **Purpose:** What is the primary goal or mission of your team?
- **Scope:** What specific tasks or projects will your team undertake?

Step 2: Identify Team Roles

- **Lion's (Dominant):** Leadership and decision-making roles.
- **Parrot's (Influential):** Creative and motivational roles.
- **Dolphin (Stable):** Operational and support roles.
- **Owl (Conscientious):** Analytical and quality-focused roles.

Step 3: Allocate Responsibilities

- **Assign roles:** Match each personality type to a role that aligns with their strengths.
- **Collaboration:** Consider how these roles will work together to achieve team objectives.

Step 4: Plan Collaboration Strategies

- **Communication:** How will team members communicate and collaborate effectively?
- **Conflict Resolution:** What strategies will be in place to address conflicts or challenges?

Step 5: Reflect and Adjust

- **Feedback:** How will you gather feedback and evaluate team performance?
- **Continuous Improvement:** What measures will be taken to enhance team cohesion and effectiveness over time?

Example Worksheet Entry:

Step	Description	Example Entry
Purpose	Develop a new mobile app to enhance user experience.	
Scope	Design, development, testing, and launch of the app.	
Lion's (Dominant)	Project Manager: Leads project planning and execution.Monthly performance reviews and user feedback analysis.	Orion
Parrot's (Influential)	UX/UI Designer: Creates intuitive and visually appealing interfaces.	Emily
Dolphin (Stable)	Quality Assurance Specialist: Ensures app functionality and user satisfaction.	Mike
Owl (Conscientious)	Data Analyst: Analyses user feedback and app performance metrics.	Sarah
Communication	Regular team meetings and updates via project management tools.	Scheduled weekly meetings, Slack for daily updates
Conflict Resolution	Mediation by project manager; encourage open dialogue and mutual understanding.	Active listening, clear communication
Feedback	Monthly performance reviews and user feedback analysis.	Surveys, app store reviews, analytics dashboard monitoring
Continuous Improvement	Agile methodology; adapt strategies based on feedback and performance metrics.	Sprint retrospectives, continuous learning opportunities

By designing your ideal team using this worksheet, you can leverage the strengths of each personality type to foster collaboration, achieve goals efficiently, and enhance overall team success.

Teamwork truly makes the dream work when you harness the diverse strengths of individual personalities effectively. By understanding how to build effective teams, drawing inspiration from real-life examples, and designing your ideal team using the provided worksheet, you can create cohesive teams that excel in achieving collective goals. Embrace diversity, foster collaboration, and celebrate achievements to ensure your team thrives and achieves success together.

Chapter 13: Romantic Entanglements: Love in the Wild

Romantic relationships often resemble a canvas splashed with various personality animals. Understanding how different personality types approach love and relationships can deepen your connection and pave the way for harmony. This chapter explores dating dynamics with different types, showcases real-life examples of famous couples, and includes a worksheet to identify your partner's type and strategies for relationship harmony.

Dating Different Types: What to Expect

Each personality type brings unique strengths and challenges to romantic relationships. Here's a glimpse into what you can expect when dating different personality types:

Lion's (Dominant):

- **Strengths:** Confident, decisive, and direct in expressing feelings and desires.
- **Challenges:** Can be seen as controlling or impatient; values independence and may struggle with vulnerability.

Parrot's (Influential):

- **Strengths:** Charismatic, fun-loving, and adventurous; enjoys spontaneous gestures and surprises.
- **Challenges:** Easily distracted, may prioritise excitement over stability; seeks validation and attention.

Dolphin (Stable):

- **Strengths:** Patient, supportive, and reliable; values loyalty and creates a nurturing environment.
- **Challenges:** Resistant to change, may avoid conflict to maintain harmony; prefers routine and predictability.

Owl (Conscientious):

- **Strengths:** Thoughtful, analytical, and detail-oriented; prioritises quality time and deep conversations.
- **Challenges:** Can be perfectionistic or overly critical; values structure and may struggle with spontaneity.

Understanding these tendencies can help navigate potential conflicts and appreciate each other's strengths in a romantic context.

Real-Life Examples: Famous Couples

Example 1: Michelle (Dolphin) and Barack Obama (Lion's)

- **Dynamic:** Michelle's stability and loyalty complement Barack's decisive leadership.
- **Strengths:** They support each other's ambitions while maintaining a strong family foundation.
- **Challenges:** Balancing Michelle's need for stability with Barack's fast-paced career demands.

Example 2: Beyoncé (Parrot's) and Jay-Z (Owl)

- **Dynamic:** Beyoncé's energy and spontaneity complement Jay-Z's thoughtful and analytical approach.
- **Strengths:** They collaborate creatively and support each other's artistic endeavours.
- **Challenges:** Managing Beyoncé's desire for excitement with Jay-Z's preference for structure and planning.

Worksheet: Identify Your Partner's Type and Strategies for Harmony

Use this worksheet to identify your partner's personality type and develop strategies for fostering harmony in your relationship.

Step 1: Identify Your Partner's Personality Type

- **Observations:** Based on their behaviour and preferences, identify which personality type best describes your partner.

Step 2: Understand Their Strengths and Challenges

- **Strengths:** What positive traits does your partner bring to the relationship?
- **Challenges:** What are the potential challenges or areas of tension?

Step 3: Strategies for Harmony

- **Communication:** How can you effectively communicate with your partner based on their personality type?
- **Compromise:** What compromises can you make to accommodate each other's needs and preferences?
- **shared Activities:** What activities can you enjoy together that align with both of your personality types?

Example Worksheet Entry:

Step	Description	Example Entry
Observations	Notice tendencies in behaviour and preferences	Sarah tends to prioritise stability and reliability in daily activities.
Personality Type	Dolphin (Stable)	
Strengths	Patient, supportive, and reliable; creates a nurturing environment.	
Challenges	Resistant to change, may avoid conflict; prefers routine and predictability.	
Communication	Use gentle and reassuring language; allow time for decision-making.	
Compromise	Respect Sarah's need for stability while encouraging small changes.	
shared Activities	Plan relaxing outings or movie nights; engage in hobbies together.	

By understanding your partner's personality type and applying these strategies, you can enhance communication, strengthen emotional bonds, and navigate challenges more effectively in your relationship.

Romantic entanglements in technicolor thrive when you appreciate and embrace the diverse personality traits of your partner. By exploring dating dynamics with different types, learning from real-life examples of famous couples, and using the provided worksheet to identify your partner's type and strategies for harmony, you can cultivate a deeper connection and create a fulfilling relationship. Celebrate each other's strengths, communicate openly, and nurture your love in all its vibrant hues.

Chapter 14: Parenting the Animal Kingdom

Parenting involves navigating the Animal spectrum of personalities that children exhibit. Understanding how different personality types develop and respond to parenting styles can significantly impact their growth and happiness. This chapter explores strategies for raising children with different personalities, shares real-life parenting challenges and solutions, and includes a worksheet to help you identify your child's type and create a tailored parenting plan.

Raising Different Types: Tailoring Your Approach

Each child is unique, and their personality influences how they perceive the world, learn, and interact. Here's how to adapt your parenting approach to different personality types:

Lion's (Dominant):

- **Approach:** Provide clear expectations and boundaries; encourage leadership and decision-making opportunities.
- **Support:** Offer challenges and goals to achieve; acknowledge their independence while guiding with firmness.

Parrot's (Influential):

- **Approach:** Foster creativity and spontaneity; allow room for exploration and social interaction.
- **Support:** Encourage their enthusiasm and curiosity; provide opportunities for them to express ideas and lead group activities.

Dolphin (Stable):

- **Approach:** Create a stable and Prepared environment; emphasise routines and consistency.
- **Support:** Offer reassurance and praise for their reliability; provide gentle guidance and patience during transitions.

Owl (Conscientious):

- **Approach:** Focus on organisation and structure; support their need for information and detail.
- **Support:** Encourage their curiosity and love for learning; provide opportunities for them to delve into their interests with depth.

Tailoring your approach based on your child's personality type can foster their strengths, support their growth areas, and strengthen your parent-child bond.

Real-Life Examples: Parenting Challenges and Solutions

Example 1: Parenting a Lion's (Dominant) Child

- **Challenge:** Managing their strong-willed nature and tendency to challenge authority.
- **Solution:** Provide clear expectations and consequences; offer choices within set boundaries to empower decision-making.

Example 2: Parenting a Parrot's (Influential) Child

- **Challenge:** Addressing their distractibility and need for constant stimulation.
- **Solution:** Engage them in structured activities; set short-term goals and celebrate achievements to maintain focus.

Example 3: Parenting a Dolphin (Stable) Child

- **Challenge:** Helping them adapt to change and embrace new experiences.
- **Solution:** Introduce changes gradually; provide reassurance and highlight the benefits of new experiences.

Example 4: Parenting a Owl (Conscientious) Child

- **Challenge:** Balancing their perfectionism and fear of failure.
- **Solution:** Encourage resilience and problem-solving skills; emphasise effort and improvement over outcomes.

Worksheet: Identify Your Child's Type and Create a Parenting Plan

Use this worksheet to identify your child's personality type and develop a personalised parenting plan that nurtures their unique qualities.

Step 1: Identify Your Child's Personality Type

- **Observations:** Notice their behaviour, preferences, and reactions in different situations.

Step 2: Understand Their Strengths and Challenges

- **Strengths:** What positive traits does your child exhibit?
- **Challenges:** What are their areas of struggle or discomfort?

Step 3: Parenting Strategies

- **Approach:** How can you adjust your parenting style to support their development?
- **Support:** What specific actions or strategies will nurture their strengths and address challenges?

Example Worksheet Entry:

Step	Description	Example Entry
Observations	Sarah prefers routine and shows empathy towards others.	
Personality Type	Dolphin (Stable)	
Strengths	Patient, reliable, and compassionate; values stability.	
Challenges	Resists change; may avoid conflict to maintain peace.	
Parenting Approach	Create a predictable routine; offer gentle guidance during transitions.	
Support	Acknowledge Sarah's reliability; encourage gradual exposure to new experiences.	

By identifying your child's personality type and implementing tailored parenting strategies, you can foster a supportive environment that promotes their growth, confidence, and emotional well-being.

Parenting the rainbow of personalities requires flexibility, empathy, and an understanding of each child's unique traits. By tailoring your approach based on their personality type, drawing insights from real-life parenting challenges and solutions, and using the provided worksheet to create a personalised parenting plan, you can nurture their strengths, support their development, and strengthen your relationship. Embrace their diversity, celebrate their individuality, and guide them with love and understanding on their journey of growth and self-discovery.

Chapter 15: The Workplace Jungle: Thriving at Work

Navigating the workplace jungle involves understanding the diverse personalities and dynamics that shape office interactions and career advancement. This chapter explores strategies for thriving in the workplace, insights into office politics, real-life examples of office dynamics, and includes a worksheet to create a personalised workplace strategy based on personalities.

Navigating Office Politics: Understanding Your Boss and Colleagues

Office politics often revolve around understanding and managing different personalities. Here's how to navigate effectively:

Understanding Your Boss:

- **Lion's (Dominant) Boss:** Values efficiency and results; prefers direct communication and decisive action.
- **Parrot's (Influential) Boss:** Charismatic and social; emphasises creativity and teamwork.
- **Dolphin (Stable) Boss:** Patient and supportive; values harmony and consistency.
- **Owl (Conscientious) Boss:** Detail-oriented and analytical; prioritises accuracy and thoroughness.

Understanding Your Colleagues:

- **Lion's (Dominant) Colleagues:** Assertive and driven; focus on achieving goals and leading initiatives.
- **Parrot's (Influential) Colleagues:** Enthusiastic and sociable; excel in collaborative projects and client interactions.
- **Dolphin (Stable) Colleagues:** Reliable and steady; thrive in supportive roles and team environments.
- **Owl (Conscientious) Colleagues:** Precise and meticulous; excel in research, analysis, and process improvement.

Example 1: Lion's (Dominant) Office Dynamics

- **Leadership Style:** Decisive and results-driven; focus on efficiency and achieving goals.
- **Team Interactions:** Clear direction and accountability; challenges to meet high expectations.

Example 2: Parrot's (Influential) Office Dynamics

- **Work Environment:** Energetic and collaborative; emphasis on creativity and social interactions.
- **Team Contributions:** Contribution to brainstorming sessions and client presentations.

Example 3: Dolphin (Stable) Office Dynamics

- **Team Support:** Reliable and consistent; maintain team cohesion and support.
- **Communication Style:** Emphasis on clarity and patience; avoid conflicts and maintain harmony.

Example 4: Owl (Conscientious) Office Dynamics

- **Task Execution:** Detailed and methodical; prioritise accuracy and adherence to procedures.
- **Role Contributions:** Contribution to data analysis and project planning.

Understanding these dynamics can help you navigate office interactions, collaborate effectively, and advance your career.

Use this worksheet to create a personalised workplace strategy that leverages the strengths of different personalities in your workplace.

Step 1: Identify Key Personalities

- **Boss:** Identify your boss's personality type and leadership style.
- **Colleagues:** Identify key colleagues' personality types and their roles within the team.

Step 2: Analyse Office Dynamics

- **Strengths:** What are the strengths of each personality type in your workplace?
- **Challenges:** What challenges or conflicts arise from different personality dynamics?

Step 3: Develop Workplace Strategy

- **Communication:** How will you adapt your communication style to interact effectively with different personalities?
- **Collaboration:** How can you leverage each personality's strengths to enhance team collaboration and productivity?
- **Career Development:** What strategies will you implement to advance your career while navigating office politics?

Example Worksheet Entry:

Step	Description	Example Entry
Boss's Personality Type	Lion's (Dominant)	
Colleague 1	Parrot's (Influential)	
Colleague 2	Dolphin (Stable)	
Colleague 3	Owl (Conscientious)	
Office Dynamics	Strengths: Lion's provides clear direction; Parrot's brings creativity.	
	Challenges: Balancing Lion's assertiveness with Dolphin's stability.	
Workplace Strategy	Communication: Use direct and concise communication with Lion's.	
	Collaboration: Engage Parrot's in brainstorming sessions; support Dolphin's reliability	
	Career Development: Seek mentorship from Owl for analytical skills development.	

By creating a personalised workplace strategy based on personalities, you can enhance your professional relationships, navigate office politics, and achieve career success.

Thriving in the workplace jungle involves understanding and adapting to the diverse personalities that shape office dynamics. By navigating office politics with insights into your boss and colleagues' personalities, drawing inspiration from real-life office dynamics, and using the provided worksheet to create a tailored workplace strategy, you can foster collaboration, advance your career, and create a positive work environment. Embrace the diversity of personalities around you, leverage their strengths, and navigate challenges with confidence and strategic insight to thrive in your professional journey.

Chapter 16: Friends of All Feathers

Maintaining friendships involves navigating the diversity of personalities that enrich our social circles. This chapter explores strategies for understanding and appreciating differences among friends, showcases real-life examples of diverse friend groups, and includes a worksheet to plan activities that cater to different personalities.

Maintaining Friendships: Understanding and Appreciating Differences

Friendships thrive when we understand and appreciate each other's unique personalities. Here's how to cultivate meaningful connections:

Understanding Different Personalities:

- **Lion's (Dominant) Friend:** Direct and assertive; values loyalty and honesty in friendships.
- **Parrot's (Influential) Friend:** Energetic and sociable; enjoys organising group activities and bringing people together.
- **Dolphin (Stable) Friend:** Reliable and supportive; values loyalty and enjoys intimate one-on-one interactions.
- **Owl (Conscientious) Friend:** Detail-oriented and thoughtful; values deep conversations and meaningful connections.

Appreciating Differences:

- **Communication:** Adapt your communication style to each friend's preferences.
- **Support:** Recognize and support each other's strengths and growth areas.
- **Respect:** Appreciate diverse perspectives and approaches to life.

Example 1: College Friend Group

- **Dynamic:** Lion's friend leads group discussions and decision-making.
- **Contribution:** Parrot's friend plans social outings and keeps the group connected.
- **Stability:** Dolphin friend offers emotional support and maintains group harmony.
- **Detail:** Owl friend organises study sessions and ensures group projects are thorough.

Example 2: Work Friend Group

- **Collaboration:** Lion's friend organises team-building activities and leads projects.
- **Enthusiasm:** Parrot's friend boosts morale with office celebrations and social events.
- **Support:** Dolphin friend offers a listening ear and practical assistance.
- **Precision:** Owl friend ensures deadlines are met and details are meticulously handled.

Worksheet: Plan Activities that Cater to Different Personalities

Use this worksheet to plan activities that cater to the diverse personalities in your friend group:

Step 1: Identify Friend's Personality Types

- **Observations:** Note each friend's behaviours, preferences, and reactions in various situations.

Step 2: Plan Activities

- **Activity:** Choose an activity that aligns with each friend's personality strengths.
- **Involvement:** Determine how each friend can contribute and enjoy the activity.

Step 3: Ensure Balance

- **Variety:** Include activities that cater to different interests and energy levels.
- **Inclusivity:** Ensure everyone feels valued and included in the planning process.

Example Worksheet Entry:

Step	Description	Example Entry
Friend 1	Lion's (Dominant): Direct and decisive; enjoys leadership roles.	John
Friend 2	Parrot's (Influential): Energetic and social; loves organising events.	Emily
Friend 3	Dolphin (Stable): Reliable and supportive; values meaningful connections.	Michael
Friend 4	Owl (Conscientious): Detail-oriented and thoughtful; enjoys deep conversations.	Sarah
Planned Activity	Activity: Weekend hiking trip	
Involvement	John plans the hiking route and logistics.	
	Emily organises group games and social activities.	
	Michael offers emotional support and ensures everyone is included.	
	Sarah researches local flora and fauna to share interesting facts.	

By planning activities that cater to different personalities, you can strengthen friendships, foster shared experiences, and create meaningful connections that celebrate diversity.

Friends of all feathers enrich our lives with their unique personalities and perspectives. By understanding and appreciating these differences, drawing inspiration from real-life diverse friend groups, and using the provided worksheet to plan activities that cater to different personalities, you can nurture strong friendships and create lasting memories. Embrace the diversity within your friend circle, celebrate each other's strengths, and enjoy the journey of growth and connection together.

Chapter 17: Personal Growth: Becoming a Chameleon

Personal growth is a journey of adaptation and transformation, where we learn to navigate and thrive in diverse environments and with different personality types. This chapter delves into strategies for adapting to various personality types, shares inspiring real-life transformation stories, and includes a worksheet to set goals for personal development.

Adapting to Different Types: Flexibility and Growth

Adapting to different personality types requires flexibility and an openness to learn and grow. Here's how to foster personal growth through adaptation:

Strategies for Adaptation:

- **Lion's (Dominant):** Be direct and assertive when needed; focus on achieving goals together.
- **Parrot's (Influential):** Engage in social interactions and support their creative ideas.
- **Dolphin (Stable):** Provide stability and patience; appreciate their reliability and support.
- **Owl (Conscientious):** Be detail-oriented and organised; value their precision and thoroughness.

Embracing Diversity:

- **Learning Opportunities:** View interactions as opportunities to understand different perspectives.
- **Communication Skills:** Develop effective communication strategies tailored to each personality type.
- **Personal Flexibility:** Cultivate adaptability and resilience in various situations.

Example 1: Career Transition

- **Story:** Sarah (formerly a Parrot's) transitioned from a creative role to project management (adopting Owl traits).
- **Transformation:** Embraced organisation and detailed planning; excelled in structured environments.

Example 2: Personal Development

- **Story:** Michael (initially Dolphin) developed assertiveness skills to lead a team project (adopting Lion's traits).
- **Transformation:** Balanced supportiveness with decisive leadership; achieved project success.

Example 3: Interpersonal Growth

- **Story:** Emily (originally Lion's) learned patience and empathy (adopting Dolphin traits) in managing diverse teams.
- **Transformation:** Improved team cohesion and morale through understanding and support.

Worksheet: Set Goals for Personal Development

Use this worksheet to set actionable goals for personal development, focusing on adapting to different personality types and fostering growth:

Step 1: Assess Current Skills and Traits

- **Strengths:** Identify your strengths in adapting to different personality types.
- **Areas for Growth:** Identify areas where you can improve in understanding and interacting with different personalities.

Step 2: Goal Setting

- **Specific Goals:** Set clear and specific goals for improving adaptability and flexibility.
- **Timeline:** Determine a timeline for achieving each goal to track progress effectively.

Step 3: Action Plan

- **Strategies:** Outline strategies and actions to achieve each goal.
- **Resources:** Identify resources or support needed to facilitate your development.

Example Worksheet Entry:

Step	Description	Example Entry
Current Skills	Strengths: Comfortable in social settings; adapt to different communication styles.	
	Areas for Growth: Improve patience in high-stress situations.	
Goal Setting	Specific Goals: Enhance ability to collaborate with Owl personalities.	
	Timeline: Achieve within the next 3 months through role-playing exercises.	
Action Plan	Strategies: Practise active listening and ask clarifying questions.	
	Resources: Seek feedback from Owl colleagues for improvement.	

By setting goals for personal development that focus on adapting to different personality types, you can enhance your interpersonal skills, foster professional growth, and contribute effectively in diverse environments.

Personal growth as a chameleon involves adapting and evolving to thrive in diverse environments and with different personality types. By embracing flexibility and growth, drawing inspiration from real-life transformation stories, and using the provided worksheet to set goals for personal development, you can navigate challenges, cultivate resilience, and achieve meaningful growth. Embrace the journey of self-discovery, celebrate progress, and continue evolving to become the best version of yourself in all aspects of life.

Chapter 18: Cultural Animals: Personality Types Around the World

Understanding how cultures influence personality types provides valuable insights into cross-cultural interactions and global perspectives. This chapter explores the impact of culture on personalities, shares real-life examples of cross-cultural interactions, and includes a worksheet to analyse cultural differences in your interactions.

Global Perspectives: How Cultures Influence Personalities

Cultural norms, traditions, and societal values shape personality development and behaviours across different regions of the world. Here's how cultures influence personality types:

Cultural Influences:

- **Individualism vs. Collectivism:** Cultures that emphasise individual achievement (e.g., United States) may foster more assertive and independent personality traits (Lion's and Parrot's). In contrast, collectivist cultures (e.g., Japan) prioritise group harmony and cooperation, nurturing stable (Dolphin) and conscientious (Owl) traits.
- **Communication Styles:** Direct communication (Lion's) may be valued in some cultures, while indirect and nuanced communication (Owl) is preferred in others.
- **Work Ethic:** Cultures with a strong work ethic may prioritise conscientious traits (Owl), while cultures emphasising leisure and social interactions may cultivate influential (Parrot's) personalities.

Real-Life Examples: Cross-Cultural Interactions

Example 1: Business Negotiations

- **Cultural Context:** Negotiating with a company in Japan (collectivist culture).
- **Approach:** Emphasise mutual benefits and long-term relationships (Dolphin), avoid aggressive tactics (Lion's).

Example 2: Travel Experiences

- **Cultural Context:** Backpacking through Southeast Asia.
- **Interaction:** Engaging with locals from different cultural backgrounds, adapting communication styles based on local norms.

Example 3: International Teams

- **Cultural Context:** Working in a multinational corporation.
- **Team Dynamics:** Recognizing and leveraging diverse personality types (Lion's, Parrot's , Dolphin, Owl) for collaborative success.

Worksheet: Analyse Cultural Differences in Your Interactions

Use this worksheet to analyse cultural differences in your interactions and develop strategies for effective communication:

Step 1: Identify Cultural Context

- **Scenario:** Describe a recent interaction with someone from a different cultural background.

Step 2: Analyse Personality and Cultural Influences

- **Observations:** Note any differences in communication styles, behaviour, or values.
- **Cultural Traits:** Identify how cultural norms may influence their personality traits (Lion's, Parrot's , Dolphin, Owl).

Step 3: Develop Communication Strategies

- **Adaptation:** How can you adapt your communication style to bridge cultural differences?
- **Respect:** What cultural values should you respect to foster positive interactions?

Example Worksheet Entry:

Step	Description	Example Entry
Cultural Context	Scenario: Business meeting with a team from South Korea.	
	Observations: Emphasis on hierarchy and respect for seniority.	
Personality Traits	Cultural Traits: Influence of collectivist values (Dolphin); respect for authority and group harmony.	
Communication	Adaptation: Use formal language and defer to senior members.	
Strategies	Respect: Acknowledge cultural norms and show appreciation for their perspectives.	

By analysing cultural differences in your interactions and developing strategies for effective communication, you can enhance cross-cultural understanding, build meaningful relationships, and navigate global contexts with sensitivity and respect.

Cultural animals shape personality types around the world, influencing behaviours, communication styles, and societal values. By understanding how cultures influence personalities, drawing inspiration from real-life cross-cultural interactions, and using the provided worksheet to analyse and adapt to cultural differences in your interactions, you can foster cultural competence, build global connections, and thrive in diverse environments. Embrace diversity, celebrate cultural richness, and continue learning to navigate the global landscape with empathy and openness.

Chapter 19: Technology and Personalities: Digital Creatures

Technology has revolutionised how we interact, presenting new challenges and opportunities influenced by personality types. This chapter explores navigating online interactions, the impact of personality types in the digital age, real-life examples from social media and remote work, and includes a worksheet to optimise your digital communication strategy.

Navigating Online Interactions: Personality Types in the Digital Age

The digital age has reshaped communication dynamics, amplifying the influence of personality types in online interactions:

Impact of Personality Types:

- **Lion's (Dominant):** Prefers concise and direct communication; may come across as assertive in emails and online discussions.
- **Parrot's (Influential):** Thrives in social media and networking platforms; enjoys sharing updates and engaging with a wide audience.
- **Dolphin (Stable):** Prefers structured and organised online environments; values online communities for support and stability.
- **Owl (Conscientious):** Pays attention to detail in digital communication; values accuracy and thoroughness in online interactions.

Challenges and Opportunities:

- **Communication Styles:** Adapting communication styles to digital platforms (e.g., email, video calls, social media).
- **Remote Work:** Leveraging technology to collaborate effectively with diverse personality types in virtual teams.
- **Social Media:** Managing online presence and interactions based on personality preferences and goals.

Example 1: Social Media Presence

- **Platform:** Instagram (Parrot's dominant).
- **Approach:** Engaging followers with vibrant content and storytelling (Influential).

Example 2: Remote Work Dynamics

- **Team Collaboration:** Utilising Slack channels (Lion's dominant).
- **Communication:** Clarifying tasks and deadlines efficiently (Conscientious).

Example 3: Online Communities

- **Support Networks:** Participating in forums and groups (Dolphin dominant).
- **Role:** Providing emotional support and practical advice within communities.

Worksheet: Optimise Your Digital Communication Strategy

Use this worksheet to assess and optimise your digital communication strategy tailored to different personality types:

Step 1: Assess Current Digital Presence

- **Platforms:** List the digital platforms you use for communication (e.g., email, social media, messaging apps).

Step 2: Analyse Personality Preferences

- **Your Traits:** Identify your own personality traits and preferences in digital communication.
- **Audience:** Consider the personality types of your audience or colleagues online.

Step 3: Develop Strategies

- **Adaptation:** How can you adapt your communication style to suit different digital platforms and personality types?
- **Engagement:** What strategies will you use to engage effectively with diverse audiences online?

Example Worksheet Entry:

Step	Description	Example Entry
Current Digital Presence	Platforms: Email, LinkedIn, Slack.	
	Your Traits: Balanced between Parrot's (Influential) and Owl (Conscientious).	
Audience	Colleagues: Mix of Lion's (Dominant) and Dolphin (Stable) personalities.	
Strategies	Adaptation: Tailor email communication to be concise and action-oriented for Lion's.	
	Engagement: Share thoughtful articles and participate actively in Slack channels for Dolphins.	

By optimising your digital communication strategy based on personality types, you can enhance online interactions, build stronger relationships, and achieve greater effectiveness in virtual environments.

Technology and personalities intersect in the digital age, influencing how we communicate, collaborate, and build relationships online. By understanding the impact of personality types in digital interactions, drawing insights from real-life examples in social media and remote work, and using the provided worksheet to optimise your digital communication strategy, you can navigate the digital landscape with clarity and effectiveness. Embrace technology as a tool for connection, adapt to digital nuances, and leverage your understanding of personality types to foster meaningful interactions and achieve your goals in the digital realm.

Chapter 20: The Future of Human Interaction

The future of human interaction is increasingly shaped by emerging technologies like AI (Artificial Intelligence), VR (Virtual Reality), and their profound impact on personalities. This chapter explores the evolving trends in human interaction, showcases real-life examples of innovations in communication, and includes a worksheet to Prepared and plan for future interactions.

Emerging Trends: AI, VR, and Their Impact on Personalities

Technological advancements are revolutionising how we interact and communicate, influencing personality development and behaviours:

AI (Artificial Intelligence):

- **Personalised Experiences:** AI-driven algorithms tailor content and recommendations based on user preferences, reflecting Parrot's (Influential) traits by enhancing engagement and social interaction.
- **Automated Assistance:** AI chatbots and virtual assistants emulate Dolphin (Stable) traits by providing reliable support and maintaining consistency in communication.

VR (Virtual Reality):

- **Immersive Environments:** VR simulations facilitate experiential learning, appealing to Owl (Conscientious) traits by offering detailed and accurate representations.
- **Virtual Collaboration:** VR meetings and conferences cater to Lion's (Dominant) traits by facilitating direct and efficient communication in virtual spaces.

Real-Life Examples: Innovations in Communication

Example 1: AI-Powered Customer Service

- **Platform:** Chatbots on customer service websites.
- **Impact:** Enhances efficiency (Lion's) and user experience (Parrot's) through personalised interactions.

Example 2: Virtual Reality in Education

- **Application:** Virtual classrooms and simulations.
- **Effect:** Facilitates immersive learning experiences (Owl) and global collaboration (Dolphin) among students.

Example 3: Telepresence in Healthcare

- **Technology:** Telemedicine and remote patient monitoring.
- **Advantage:** Provides accessible healthcare (Dolphin) and accurate diagnostics (Owl) remotely.

Worksheet: Predict and Plan for Future Interactions

Use this worksheet to anticipate and strategize for future interactions influenced by emerging technologies:

Step 1: Identify Emerging Technologies

- **Technologies:** List AI and VR applications relevant to your field or personal interests.

Step 2: Assess Potential Impacts

- **Personality Traits:** Prepared how these technologies might influence different personality traits (Lion's, Parrot's , Dolphin, Owl).
- **Scenarios:** Imagine scenarios where AI and VR could enhance or challenge interactions.

Step 3: Develop Strategic Responses

- **Adaptation:** How will you adapt your communication and interaction style in response to these technologies?
- **Opportunities:** Identify opportunities to leverage AI and VR to enhance productivity, creativity, and collaboration.

Example Worksheet Entry:

Step	Description	Example Entry
Emerging Technologies	Technologies: AI-driven analytics and VR conferencing tools.	
Assess Potential Impacts	Personality Traits: AI enhances efficiency (Lion's); VR promotes immersive learning (Owl).	
	Scenarios: AI chatbot for customer service (Parrot's), VR training simulations (Dolphin).	
Strategic Responses	Adaptation: Develop AI strategies for personalised customer interactions.	
	Opportunities: Implement VR for global team collaboration and training programs.	

By predicting and planning for future interactions influenced by AI, VR, and other emerging technologies, you can adapt proactively, harness their potential, and navigate evolving communication landscapes effectively.

The future of human interaction is marked by transformative technologies like AI and VR, reshaping how we communicate, collaborate, and innovate. By understanding their impact on personality traits, drawing inspiration from real-life innovations in communication, and using the provided worksheet to Prepared and plan for future interactions, you can embrace technological advancements, leverage their benefits, and navigate challenges with foresight and adaptability. Embrace the future of human interaction with curiosity and readiness to evolve, ensuring your interactions remain meaningful and impactful in a rapidly changing world.

1. Case Studies and Success Stories

Case studies and success stories play a crucial role in illustrating how understanding personality types can lead to effective outcomes in various contexts.

Business Context:

Case Study: Leadership Effectiveness

- **Scenario:** A multinational corporation was facing challenges with team cohesion and productivity. Through personality assessments, it was discovered that the executive team was composed primarily of Lion's (Dominant) and Owl (Conscientious) personalities, leading to clashes in decision-making styles.

- **Application:** By implementing tailored communication strategies and fostering mutual understanding of each personality type's strengths, the company successfully improved collaboration, streamlined decision-making processes, and boosted employee morale. This resulted in a significant increase in project delivery efficiency and overall profitability.

Success Story: Sales and Customer Relations

- **Scenario:** A sales team struggled to connect with clients effectively, resulting in missed sales targets. Through personality assessments, it was identified that the team members predominantly exhibited Parrot's (Influential) and Lion's (Dominant) traits.
- **Application:** By training sales representatives to adapt their communication styles to match client preferences (Owl for detailed information, Parrot's for engaging storytelling), the team saw a notable increase in client engagement, satisfaction ratings, and ultimately, exceeded sales targets for consecutive quarters.

Case Study: Couple Counselling

- **Scenario:** A couple sought counselling due to recurring misunderstandings and communication breakdowns. Personality assessments revealed that one partner leaned towards Dolphin (Stable) traits, preferring routine and predictability, while the other exhibited Parrot's (Influential) traits, valuing spontaneity and social interactions.

- **Application:** Armed with insights into their differing personality preferences, the couple learned to communicate more effectively, appreciate each other's perspectives, and proactively compromise on activities and decision-making processes. This led to a strengthened bond, reduced conflicts, and a renewed sense of partnership.

Education Context:

Success Story: Classroom Dynamics

- **Scenario:** A teacher struggled to engage a diverse group of students with varying learning preferences and behavioural tendencies. Personality assessments revealed a mix of Dolphin (Stable), Parrot's (Influential), and Owl (Conscientious) traits among the students.

- **Application:** By implementing differentiated teaching strategies tailored to each personality type (interactive group activities for Parrot's, detailed study guides for Owls, consistent routines for Dolphins), the teacher created a more inclusive and conducive learning environment. This resulted in improved academic performance, enhanced student participation, and a positive classroom atmosphere.

Personality Assessment for Technology Interaction

Instructions: Answer each question honestly to determine which personality traits **(Lion's, Parrot's , Dolphin, Owl)** resonate most with you in the context of technology interaction.

1. **Decision-Making Style:**
   - When faced with a problem, I prefer to:
     - a) Quickly make a decision and take action (Lion's).
     - b) Discuss with others and seek consensus (Parrot's).
     - c) Take time to weigh options and consider all possibilities (Owl).
     - d) Maintain stability and avoid unnecessary risks (Dolphin).

2. **Communication Preference:**
   - In digital conversations, I tend to:
     - a) Get straight to the point and focus on facts (Lion's).
     - b) Engage others with enthusiasm and share personal anecdotes (Parrot's).
     - c) Provide detailed explanations and ask clarifying questions (Owl).
     - d) Listen attentively and provide emotional support (Dolphin).

3. **Social Media Use:**
   - When using social media, I am most likely to:
     - a) Share updates related to achievements and goals (Lion's).
     - b) Interact with a wide range of people and join conversations (Parrot's).
     - c) Share informative articles and thoughtful insights (Owl).
     - d) Support friends and maintain connections (Dolphin).

4. **Technology Adaptation:**
   - When learning new technology or software, I:
     - a) Prefer to dive in and explore features independently (Lion's).
     - b) Enjoy exploring new features and sharing discoveries with others (Parrot's).
     - c) Follow instructions meticulously to understand all functions (Owl).
     - d) Appreciate user-friendly interfaces and clear instructions (Dolphin).

5. **Remote Work Preferences:**
   - In a remote work setting, I prioritise:
     - a) Setting clear goals and deadlines (Lion's).
     - b) Staying connected with colleagues through frequent updates (Parrot's).
     - c) Ensuring accuracy and completeness in tasks (Owl).
     - d) Maintaining regular routines and stable work patterns (Dolphin).

6. **Problem-Solving Approach:**
   - When faced with a technical issue, I am more likely to:
     - a) Take immediate action to troubleshoot and find a solution (Lion's).
     - b) Discuss the issue with others and gather different perspectives (Parrot's).
     - c) Analyse the problem systematically and seek underlying causes (Owl).
     - d) Remain patient and seek guidance from reliable sources (Dolphin).

Scoring:

- Count the number of a), b), c), and d) responses for each question.
- The personality type with the highest number of responses indicates your primary inclination in technology interaction.

This assessment sheet helps individuals identify their predominant personality traits (Lion's, Parrot's , Dolphin, Owl) in the context of technology interaction. Understanding these preferences can guide how they approach digital communication, adapt to new technologies, and anticipate their interaction style in future technological landscapes.

Personality Assessment: Discover Your Animal Personality

This assessment helps you identify your dominant personality type: Lion's (Dominant), Parrot's (Influential), Dolphin (Stable), or Owl (Conscientious). Answer the following questions honestly based on how you typically think, feel, and behave. At the end of the assessment, tally your scores to see which animal represents your personality.

Instructions:

For each statement, rate how much you agree on a scale of 1 to 5:

1 = Strongly Disagree

2 = Disagree

3 = Neutral

4 = Agree

5 = Strongly Agree

Statement	1	2	3	4	5
I enjoy taking charge and leading others					
I feel energised by social interactions and meeting new people.					
I am patient and enjoy supporting others.					
I pay close attention to details and prefer tasks to be done accurately.					
I thrive in competitive environments and enjoy challenges.					
I am enthusiastic and often bring excitement to group activities.					
I value harmony and work to avoid conflicts.					
I prefer to plan and organise my tasks systematically.					
I am decisive and often make quick decisions.					
I am persuasive and can easily influence others.					
I am reliable and others often count on me for support.					
I approach problems with a logical and analytical mindset.					
I enjoy setting and achieving ambitious goals.					
I am creative and enjoy thinking outside the box.					
I am a good listener and people often come to me for advice.					
I prefer to gather all necessary information before making a decision.					
I am assertive and confident in expressing my opinions.					
I enjoy being the centre of attention and engaging with others.					
I am dependable and consistent in my actions.					
I value accuracy and precision in my work.					

Scoring:

1. Add up your scores for the following statements to find your total for each animal:
   - **Lion's (Dominant):** 1, 5, 9, 13, 17
   - **Parrot's (Influential):** 2, 6, 10, 14, 18
   - **Dolphin (Stable):** 3, 7, 11, 15, 19
   - **Owl (Conscientious):** 4, 8, 12, 16, 20
2. Your highest total indicates your dominant personality type.

Example Scoring Table:

Personality Type	Statement Scores	Total
Lion's (Dominant)	1, 5, 9, 13, 17	
Parrot's (Influential)	2, 6, 10, 14, 18	
Dolphin (Stable)	3, 7, 11, 15, 19	
Owl (Conscientious)	4, 8, 12, 16, 20	

Results Interpretation:

- **Lion's (Dominant):** You are a natural leader, decisive, and thrive on challenges.
- **Parrot's (Influential):** You are energetic, sociable, and enjoy inspiring others.
- **Dolphin (Stable):** You are patient, reliable, and value harmony and support.
- **Owl (Conscientious):** You are detail-oriented, analytical, and value accuracy.

Understanding your dominant personality type can help you leverage your strengths and improve interactions with others. Use this insight to navigate different scenarios more effectively, whether in personal relationships, at work, or in social settings. Enjoy your journey to self-discovery and better communication!

Blank Worksheet Entry:

Step	Description	Example Entry

To Our Dear Readers

Thank you for taking the time to dive into the Animal world of personalities with us! Your investment in understanding yourself and those around you is a fantastic step toward enhancing your communication, relationships, and overall personal growth.

We hope that the insights, exercises, and examples in this book have not only entertained you but also provided practical tools for your everyday interactions. Remember, the journey of self-discovery and improvement is ongoing, and every step you take brings you closer to becoming the best version of yourself.

If you enjoyed this book and are eager to explore more, check out my other works on Amazon. Just search for "Orion Windsor" and you'll find a range of books designed to inspire and guide you. Additionally, if you're interested in delving deeper into topics like personal development and holistic healing, tune into my podcast, "Quanttum Healing," available on Spotify. It's packed with insights, expert interviews, and tips to support your journey.

Thank you once again for your commitment to personal growth and for choosing this book as a part of your journey. Stay curious, stay motivated, and keep exploring the vibrant tapestry of human personalities!

Warm regards,

Orion Windsor

Welcome to My Notes (Thoughts and Feelings)

Welcome to My Notes (Thoughts and Feelings)

Welcome to My Notes (Thoughts and Feelings)

Welcome to My Notes (Thoughts and Feelings)

Welcome to My Notes (Thoughts and Feelings)

Welcome to My Notes (Thoughts and Feelings)

Welcome to My Notes (Thoughts and Feelings)